Accelerating Catch-up

Accelerating Catch-up

*Tertiary Education for Growth in
Sub-Saharan Africa*

THE WORLD BANK
Washington, D.C.

1818 H Street NW
Washington DC 20433
Telephone: 202-473-1000
Internet: www.worldbank.org
E-mail: feedback@worldbank.org

ISBN-13: 978-0-8213-7738-3
eISBN: 978-0-8213-7739-0
DOI: 10.1596/978-0-8213-7738-3

Library of Congress Cataloging-in-Publication Data

Accelerating catch-up: tertiary education for growth in SSA / AFTHD (World Bank), DECRG (World Bank).
    p. cm.
    Includes bibliographical references and index.
    ISBN 978-0-8213-7738-3—ISBN 978-0-8213-7739-0 (e-book)
    1. Education, Higher—Economic aspects—Africa, Sub-Saharan. 2. Economic development—Africa, Sub-Saharan—Effect of education on. I. World Bank. AFTHD. II. World Bank. DECRG.
LC67.68.A357A23 2008
33S.4'337868—dc22

                                                                    2008035536

Cover photo: © Wei Yan/Masterfile
Cover design: Candace Roberts, Quantum Think, Philadelphia, PA, United States

Contents

Figures

Tables

Foreword

The revival of economic growth across Sub-Saharan African (SSA) since the beginning of the millennium is a heartening development. Sustaining it over the indefinite future is both a necessity and a challenge of the first order. It is a necessity because this is the only way that poverty can be steadily reduced and progress made toward achieving the Millennium Development Goals (MDGs). It is a challenge because many African countries are some distance from meeting the preconditions for stable growth and are faced with tightening constraints on growth arising from higher prices for energy and food, climate change, and stiff entry barriers to the global markets for manufactures. The challenge can—and in fact must—be met because a weakening economic performance that threatens a return to the economic conditions of the 1990s would be a great human tragedy. But maintaining the current momentum, and accelerating growth wherever possible, requires measures that will substantially enhance economic competitiveness and nurture expansion of new tradable activities. To realize these objectives, countries in SSA must harness both more capital and more knowledge. The two are complements. SSA needs to invest heavily in physical infrastructure and productive capacity. However, maximizing productivity and achieving competitiveness will depend upon success in augmenting human capital and raising its quality.

The key to economic success in a globalized world lies increasingly in how effectively a country can assimilate the available knowledge and build comparative advantage in selected areas with good growth prospects, and in how it can enlarge the comparative advantage by pushing the frontiers of technology through innovation. Capital is a necessary handmaiden, but the arbiter of economic success—even survival—in the world today is the capacity to mobilize knowledge and to use it to the fullest.

African countries have gone far in achieving high levels of literacy and raising primary enrollments, and they are increasingly seeking to improve learning outcomes as well. This progress is providing a foundation for future development. Now it is necessary to move quickly to acquire the higher-order skills and expertise that will allow African countries to add value to existing economic activities and enter new industries and services.

This volume lucidly spells out the case for more knowledge-intensive growth, which demands increasing attention to secondary and, most important, postsecondary education. Despite rising enrollment in tertiary-level institutions, the numbers of students graduating are pitifully small. And despite reform efforts, the quality remains well below par. However, change for the better is in the air, and improved economic prospects provide both the resources and the opportunity to forge ahead. The need for urgency, the pathways to skills-based development, and the policies that African countries can marshal in order to generate tertiary-level skills are all given their due in this thoughtful and timely book.

My hope is that publication of this volume will help engage all relevant stakeholders—at the national and regional levels in Africa, and between African countries and their development partners—in purposeful dialogue about the need for, and challenge of, reform as well as for investments in education so that countries can acquire the higher-order skills and expertise they will need for successful competition in today's global economy. As with any transformation, country conditions will matter in the design of the reform package, and the process will often involve difficult changes and trade-offs and sustained efforts to achieve results. Supporting African countries in this process is an important task for the development community, one in which collaboration across agencies, and alignment with country strategies that are informed by global good practice and are led by national authorities, can contribute to Africa's economic and social development in the coming years.

Yaw Ansu
Director, Human Development, Africa Region

Acknowledgments

Shahid Yusuf, William Saint, and Kaoru Nabeshima wrote the main report, drawing upon 16 background studies of tertiary education in Sub-Saharan Africa, which included analyses of export diversification by Vandana Chandra, and university-industry linkages by a number of African researchers. Yaw Ansu recognized the need for this report and supported it throughout. Jee-Peng Tan initiated the work and supervised the team that prepared the report. Peter Materu managed the task and led the consultations with the External Advisory Panel. Petra Righetti provided research, organizational, and administrative support. Marinella Yadao assisted with the production of the manuscript.

External Advisory Panel Members

Philip Altbach	Monan Professor of Higher Education, Boston College, United States
Jean-Eric Aubert	World Bank, France
Robert Bates	Professor, Harvard University, United States
Kerry Bolognese	Program Officer, National Association of State Universities and Land-Grant Colleges, United States
George Bugliarello	Foreign Secretary, National Academy of Engineering, United States
Arlindo Chilundo	Former Higher Education Coordinator, Mozambique
Carl Dahlman	Professor, Georgetown University, United States
Gerardo Della Paolera	Professor and Director, The American University of Paris, France
Philip Griffiths	President, Institute for Advanced Studies, United States
Gudmund Hernes	Professor, Norwegian School of Management, Norway
Jeroen Huisman	Director, European Center for Higher Education Management, United Kingdom

Piyushi Kotecha	Chief Executive Officer, Southern African Regional Universities Association, Johannesburg, South Africa
David Lindauer	Professor, Wellesley College, United States
Inacio Calvino Maposse	Higher Education Coordinator, Mozambique
Hon. Venancio Massingue	Minister of Science and Technology, Mozambique
Peter McPherson	President, National Association of State Universities and Land-Grant Colleges, United States
Bonaventure Mvé-Ondo	Vice-recteur à la regionalization, Agence universitaire de la francophonie
John Mugabe	Adviser on Science and Technology, The New Partnership for Africa's Development, Johannesburg, South Africa
Ahmadou Lamine Ndiaye	Vice President, National Academy of Sciences and Technologies, Senegal
Njuguna Ng'ethe	Professor, University of Nairobi, Kenya
Beatrice Njenga	Head of the Education Division of the Commission of the Africa Union, Nairobi, Kenya
Dorothy Njeuma	Rector, University of Yaounde I, Cameroon
Chacha Nyaigotti-Chacha	Executive Secretary, Inter-University Council for East Africa, Kampala, Uganda
Daniel O'Hare	Retired Chair, Skills Development Council, Ireland
Peter Okebukola	Former Executive Secretary, National Universities Commission, Abuja, Nigeria
Jan Sadlak	Director, European Centre for Higher Education, Bucharest, Romania
Akilagpa Sawyerr	Secretary General, Association of African Universities, Accra, Ghana
Juma Shabani	Director, United Nations Educational, Scientific, and Cultural Organization, Mali
Law Song Seng	Former Chairman of the Institute of Technical Education, Singapore
Sibry Tapsoba	Manager Higher Education, Science, and Technology, African Development Bank,
Ulrich Teichler	Professor, University of Kassel, Kassel Germany

Acronyms

AERC	African Economic Research Consortium
AfDB	African Development Bank
AIDS	Acquired immune deficiency syndrome
ANSTI	African Network of Scientific and Technical Institutions
ASTI	Agricultural Science and Technology Indicators
CAMES	Conseil Africain et Malgache pour l'Enseignement Supérieur
CEPES	Centre Européen pour l'Enseignement Supérieur
CGIAR	Consultative Group on International Agricultural Research
CIRAD	Centre de coopération internationale en recherche agronomique pour le développement
CODESRIA	Council for the Development of Social Science Research in Africa
COMESA	Common Market for Southern and Eastern Africa
CONFEMEN	Conference of Ministers of Education of French-speaking Countries
CRUFAOCI	Council of Francophone University Rectors from Africa and the Indian Ocean
ECOWAS	Economic Community of West African States

EXPY	Rodrik-Hausmann score of export sophistication and competitiveness
FINNIDA	Finnish International Development Agency
GCI	Global competitiveness index
GDP	Gross domestic product
GER	Gross enrollment ratio
HIV	Human immunodeficiency virus
ICA	Investment Climate Assessment
ICHEFAP	International Comparative Higher Education Finance and Accessibility
ICT	Information and Communications Technology
IFAD	International Fund for Agricultural Development
IRD	International Relief and Development
ISCED	International standard classification of education
IT	Information technology
IUCEA	Inter-University Council for East Africa
K4D	Knowledge for Development Index
MDGs	Millennium Development Goals
MVA	Manufacturing value added
NASULGC	National Association of State Universities and Land-Grant Colleges
NEPAD	The New Partnership for Africa's Development
NIS	National innovation system
NORAD	Norwegian Agency for Development
ODA	Official development assistance
OECD	Organisation for Economic Co-operation and Development
PPP	Purchasing power parity
PRSPs	Poverty Reduction Strategy Papers
PTA	Preferential Trade Area
R&D	Research and development
RUFORUM	Regional Universities Forum for Capacity Building in Agriculture
SADC	South African Development Community
SAREC	Department for Research Cooperation of the Swedish International Development Cooperation Agency
SARUA	Southern African Regional Universities Association
S&E	Science and engineering
S&T	Science and technology

SIDA	Swedish International Development Cooperation Agency
SMEs	Small and medium enterprises
SMIs	Small and medium industries
SSA	Sub-Saharan Africa
TAMA	Technology Advanced Metropolitan Area
TEFT	Technology Transfer from Research Institute to SMEs
TLO	Technology licensing offices
UNCTAD	United Nations Commission on Trade and Development
UNECA	United Nations Economic Commission for Africa
UNESCO	United Nations Educational, Scientific and Cultural Organization
UNIDO	United Nations Industrial Development Organization
USAID	U.S. Agency for International Development
USHEPiA	University Science, Humanities and Engineering Partnerships in Africa
WFP	World Food Programme
WHO	World Health Organization

Executive Summary

Growth in gross domestic product (GDP) in Sub-Saharan Africa (SSA) has accelerated from an average annual rate of 2.0 percent during the 1990s to over 6.0 percent during 2002-07. This remarkable economic turnaround is the result of increasing macroeconomic stability, of reforms that have whittled away market imperfections and reduced trade barriers, and most consequentially, of rapidly increasing global demand for the natural resource-based commodities exported by Sub-Saharan countries. This swelling demand, fueled by the expansion of the leading Asian economies, has improved the terms of trade for some countries in SSA, and substantially increased the transfer of resources from abroad, while stimulating investment in the primary sector, infrastructure, and urban housing and services. Coming after more than two decades of stagnation, the recent growth spurt in economic performance is a welcome development.

But if this growth surge is to evolve into a virtuous spiral that stimulates even higher and sustained growth rates in a substantial number of African countries, a significant increase in investment in physical and human capital is needed over an extended period. This report argues that there is an urgent need for countries in SSA to acquire the capabilities that will spawn new industries that create more productive jobs, multiple linkages, and a wider range of exports. The desired capabilities derive from investment in physical assets, such as infrastructure and productive facilities, as well as in institutions and human capital. We have stressed human capital in this report, because in the context of SSA, it is arguably the stepping-stone to a viable and growth-promoting industrial system. Physical investment and a variety of market and non-market institutions are important complements. But as experience has shown, the former cannot be efficiently utilized or maintained where technical and managerial skills are in short supply, and the latter cannot be engineered or implemented when human capital is desperately scarce and of questionable quality. The salience of human capital is increased by the necessity of moving up the technological ladder so as to diversify into higher value, knowledge- and research-intensive activities with good longer-term demand prospects, which promise better returns and are less subject to competitive pressures. However, this is not the only reason why human capital is becoming central to SSA's growth strategy. Human capital, effectively harnessed, would enable African economies to increase allocative efficiency and maximize the returns from (initially) limited supplies of physical capital. Moreover, it is only through the application of knowledge that African countries will be able to cope with potentially crippling threats from prevalent diseases, expanding youthful and urbanizing populations, and impending climate change.

Africa's stock of human capital with secondary- and tertiary-level skills is comparatively small.[1] Its quality is highly variable, and the accumulation of skills in some countries is dampened by mortality arising from infectious diseases and by emigration of many of the most talented. Only by raising the rate of investment in human capital can the region reach and sustain the level of economic performance it needs to generate an adequate volume of employment for expanding populations, to achieve various Millennium Development Goal (MDG) targets, and to narrow the economic gap between SSA and other developing regions. The report identifies and analyzes the challenges that countries in SSA face in seeking to achieve these aspirations. It underscores the role of tertiary education in meeting these challenges and, by drawing on African and international experience, it indicates the policy steps that will enable African tertiary institutions to support knowledge-intensive growth strategies.

The Rising Salience of Tertiary Education

A wealth of recent research has convincingly established the relationship of the accumulation of physical capital and total factor productivity (the combined increase in the productivity of capital and labor) to growth. The two are interrelated. Capital contributes directly to growth through embodied technological change that enhances productivity. Because technological change is increasingly skill biased, human capital complements the creation of productive capacity. Human capital affects growth through multiple channels: by increasing allocative efficiency and the efficiency with which assets are managed, utilized, and maintained; through entrepreneurship; and through innovation, which raises productivity, unlocks new investment opportunities, and enhances export competitiveness. The spread of information and communication technology (ICT) is further strengthening the demand for skills and, in particular, for skills of higher quality.

Private and social returns to education have consistently been high. Earlier research found larger returns for primary education than for secondary or tertiary education. However, the picture is changing and the returns to tertiary education have risen appreciably. Private returns to tertiary education in low-income countries are now frequently on par with the returns from primary education. Each additional year of education can yield 10 percent to 15 percent returns in the form of higher wages. Furthermore, micro studies are identifying links between skills and higher productivity at the level of the firm, while research using macro data is showing that research and development (R&D) raises productivity, as does the quality of education (measured by middle school test scores). In fact, a one-year increase in average tertiary education levels would raise annual GDP growth in SSA by 0.39 percentage points and increase the long-run steady state level of African GDP per capita by 12 percent. This may be a result of the competitive pressures released by the integration of the global economy, the acceleration of technological change, and the skill intensity of newer production methods and services.

By raising the level of education and its quality, countries in SSA may be able to stimulate innovation, promote the diversification of products and services, and maximize returns from capital assets through more efficient allocation and management. In the face of competition from South and East Asian countries, a more skill-intensive route to development could provide both resource-rich and resource-poor countries an avenue for raising domestic value added.

How the World Bank's Approach Is Changing

The World Bank has long championed education, and continues to view the Millennium Development Goal of universal primary education as a necessary objective for developing countries. However, for all the reasons spelled out above, and in light of recent trends in technology, neglecting tertiary education could seriously jeopardize longer-term growth prospects of SSA countries, while slowing progress toward MDGs, many of which require tertiary-level training to implement. While affirming the continuing importance of primary and secondary education—which shape the overall productivity of the labor force and constitute the stepping-stones to quality higher education, this study concentrates on the tertiary education sector only, complementing recent World Bank reports that analyze other major components of the education system (Bruns, Mingat, Rakotomalala 2003; World Bank 2008a; Johanson and Adams 2004). The report seeks to inform discussion and policy making as African countries consider the types of innovations needed to build tertiary education systems equal to the global economic challenges these countries are and will be facing.

A more knowledge-intensive approach to development is emerging as an attractive option for many African countries. In fact, it is possibly the only route that could permit sustained, outward-oriented development. Even though social and political demands press for expansion of enrollment at public tertiary institutions, these must be balanced against the need to raise the relevance of education and research, and by targeting the production of those technical skills and areas of applied research that will promote competitive industries. Too rapid an increase in enrollments, as has happened in the recent past, has eroded quality and is undermining the contribution of tertiary education to growth.

Thus, the inability to manage the expansion of enrollments in traditional public sector tertiary institutions in ways that preserve educational quality and provide sustainability in financing is a major obstacle for nations seeking to join the knowledge economy. Arguably, private universities, technical institutes, nonresident community colleges, and distance learning programs could offer financially viable avenues for continued enrollment expansion, while public institutions go through a period of consolidation that concentrates on boosting quality, reinvigorating research, and solidifying graduate programs. In the long run, traditional delivery systems for tertiary education based on residential campuses and face-to-face teaching may need to be supplemented by or transformed into different delivery models if sustainable expansion of postsecondary enrollments is to take place.

Why Tertiary Education and Its Quality Matter

There are at least four reasons for prioritizing educational quality over quantity at the higher levels of education. First, it substantially increases the effect of education spending on economic outcomes—quality is more closely correlated with growth. Second, there can be little doubt that workers with higher quality cognitive, as well as technical, communication, and team skills, are better able to assimilate technology, to push the knowledge frontier, to work in groups, and to make efficient decisions. These are the "capacity" skills that SSA badly needs if it is to build the requisite technological capability for competitiveness, and to serve as the basis for innovation in applied research in fields such as engineering and the biosciences. The latter, for example, hold out the promise of more productive, nutritious, and better adapted varieties of crops, new food processing technologies, new medicines, new biofuels, and new materials. Such products and processes will enable SSA to transition into a higher growth trajectory that facilitates progress toward MDGs in poverty reduction, food security, education, and health. Third, tertiary institutions that are equipped to impart quality education and conduct relevant applied research are also more likely to cultivate multiple linkages with industry and to stimulate knowledge-based development through a variety of proven channels, only a few of which are currently utilized in Africa. Tertiary-level institutions in SSA, along with research institutes, have an increasingly vital role to play in helping industry gain access to and leverage advances in domestic and foreign technology and diversify into a broader range of products. Fourth, as many countries in Africa and other regions are finding, simply expanding tertiary education is no panacea. Where its quality is low and there is a mismatch between skills and demand, many graduates have difficulty finding employment. Tertiary institutions need to be better attuned to market demands for both near-term needs, as well as to provide students with the solid grounding in basic disciplines that will enable them to acquire new skills in the future if market demands shift, as they are likely to do. This will not eliminate frictional unemployment of graduates, but under conditions of macroeconomic stability, they could reduce the waste of public resources and human capital that it entails.

Flight of Human Capital

The mismatch between skills and demand, starting salaries that are below the expectations of graduates, few job opportunities, and unsettled political conditions, are also responsible for the emigration of tertiary graduates from African countries, and the reluctance of students who study overseas to return to their home countries. The brain drain continually subtracts some of the more highly qualified individuals from the domestic pools of human capital. Net emigration from SSA was 0.57 million in 1995; fell to 0.29 million in 2000; and then rose to 1.07 million in 2005. An estimated one-third of these were university graduates. Moreover, while their remittances bolster household consumption and are a valuable lifeline for poorer families, in some instances, they exert upward pressure on exchange rates, making it harder for producers in the affected countries to enter export markets for low-end manufactured goods and tradable services. While acknowledging the cost imposed by the brain drain, we underscore the longer-term view. The option to migrate provides incentives to acquire specialized education, and the expanding diasporas of knowledge workers from Africa are a potential reservoir of talent and entrepreneurship that some countries are beginning to tap into through Internet-based collaboration, for example. They are also a source of US$22 billion in remittances for SSA. Moreover, if countries are able to maintain their performance, and attractive job opportunities multiply, talent has a tendency to flow back.

Regional Solutions

Some difficulties in equilibrating the market for tertiary-level skills might be most effectively dealt with through regionally coordinated interventions that shape the supply of graduates and the demand for skills. In view of the small size of many of the countries and the limited resources at their disposal, regional partnerships among groups of countries would be both cost-effective and more likely to help build institutions that have the scale and the finances to provide specialized training and conduct strategic research. In many cases, the best route to establishing a regional center of excellence may be through the development of a strong national institution that progressively creates a regional sphere of attraction as its reputation grows. As economic liberalism and competitiveness spread around the globe, regional trade and development pacts among African countries, such as the Southern African Development Community (SADC), the Common Market for Southern and Eastern Africa (COMESA), and the Economic Community of West African States (ECOWAS), have been gaining political support and institutional capacity. They could provide a basis for coordinating regional approaches to the strengthening of tertiary education systems. But for regional initiatives to have their desired impact, procedures and institutional capacities that enable student mobility within the region and to ascertain the equivalence of degrees among countries will be required.

Shortcomings of Tertiary Institutions and Past Policies

Efforts to reform tertiary education systems to enhance quality and increase the supply of science and engineering (S&E) graduates in particular, have been ongoing in most African countries since the 1990s, and heartening evidence of progress is visible in some countries and within numerous tertiary institutions. Still, no country can convincingly claim to have put its tertiary education on sound long-term footing, and no university from SSA is represented in the ranks of the top 200 universities in the world. The nature of the reforms required has been frequently rehearsed and cases of successful individual institutional reforms have been documented. But systemwide reform efforts have fallen short in three important respects.

First, very few countries have adequately recognized the increasing skill intensity of development, or viewed tertiary education reform as integral to their economic growth strategies. The connection of national economic development strategies with the type, quality, and number of tertiary graduates needed to implement them has yet to be made. For this reason, there has been insufficient headway toward defining development objectives for tertiary education, identifying the policy actions necessary to achieve these, imposing a time frame for their implementation, and monitoring progress.

Second, with technology absorption and technological capabilities becoming the keys to industrial competitiveness and to gains in factor productivity, the flagship universities in each country have yet to nurture problem-oriented research that would interact with and contribute to the leading economic subsectors. This research should be framed to provide the basis for technological catch-up and the foundation of a national innovation system. East Asian economies are all committed to knowledge-based development because they now see advances in technological capabilities as inseparable from growing economies. SSA cannot afford inaction on this front, and time is increasingly of the essence in a globally competitive economy.

Third, complementary organizational structures in SSA countries are still not in place to strengthen technological capabilities. Various countries have adopted different forms to suit their needs. For instance, India created the Council of Scientific and Industrial Research, which is an independent body under the prime minister, tasked with promoting research in areas with commercial promise, building R&D capabilities, and disseminating research findings (World Bank Institute 2007). The Fundacion

Chile has achieved fame in Latin America through its successful efforts to start up innovative enterprises in association with the private sector, assist them in accessing and adapting technologies, and, more broadly, helping to create an infrastructure for the acquisition and transfer of technologies. Other examples include the Malaysian Agricultural Research and Development Institute, which works with the Malaysian Palm Oil Board and the universities to develop new products based on Malaysia's major tree crops (Rasiah 2006). Finland has set up Tekes—the Finnish Funding Agency for Technology and Innovation—a public funded body specifically for R&D conducted by tertiary education institutions, firms, and research institutes. Through its funding of linked strategic priorities, it steers and coordinates R&D activities conducted by various entities.

The Present in Perspective

Tertiary education in Africa has come a long way in the past two decades. Enrollments have expanded by 8.7 percent annually, compared to 5.1 percent for the world as a whole, and have tripled since 1990, to almost 4 million students. The number of tertiary institutions now surpasses 650 (some 200 public and 450 private). The private sector has established itself as an important part of the tertiary system, accounting for 18 percent of enrollments in the region. Women's access to tertiary education has improved markedly, from one out of six students in 1990 to roughly one out of three today. More diversified tertiary systems have been put in place through the creation of specialized institutions dedicated to agriculture, teacher training, science and technology, and women's education. Capacities for distance education have been developed within existing institutions, as well as through open universities set up solely for distance learning. One-third of African nations have now introduced quality assurance agencies, and 10 countries have also established oversight agencies or "buffer bodies" to manage tertiary system development. As a result, maturing tertiary education systems now characterize numerous African countries.

But these achievements have come at a high price. On average, SSA countries now spend 18.2 percent of government budgets on education, a share that approaches the upper limits of what is generally considered to be feasible. The nations of the region also allocate 20 percent of their education budgets to tertiary education, an amount that borders on the high end of what is accepted as good practice. At the same time, household surveys indicate that families spend a significant amount of their incomes on education, and persistently high food and fuel prices may squeeze these possibilities in the future.

Despite this effort, enrollment growth has outpaced financing capabilities, and in many cases resulted in deteriorating educational quality. Public expenditure per tertiary student has fallen from US$6,800 in 1980, to US$1,200 in 2002, and recently averaged just US$981 in 33 low-income SSA countries. The ratio of academic staff to students has fallen significantly, producing overcrowded classrooms and unrelenting workloads for teaching staff. This has contributed to a severe crisis in staffing, compounded by retirements (with many more to come), brain drain, attrition due to AIDS, poor working conditions, and insufficient output from postgraduate programs. These dynamics have forced some institutions to begin hiring bachelor of arts degree holders to teach undergraduates, and have generally hobbled research output across the continent. However, despite the expansion in enrollment, only 5 percent of the relevant age cohort is receiving tertiary education.

The future, therefore, promises no immediate relief from these pressures as a rising tide of graduates from basic education—testament to the success of a decade of Education for All efforts—is now jostling for entry into secondary education, and will soon be banging on the doors of tertiary institutions. Left unchecked, a continuation of current trends will produce a further tripling of tertiary enrollments by 2020. Enrollments will be fueled by record numbers of youth as a demographic "bulge" works its way through the SSA education system in the decade ahead. The interplay of these two factors will generate intense social pressure for access to higher levels of education, which most elected politicians within Africa's relatively new democracies will find impossible to ignore. As noted above, both the state and households are already at or near the limits of what they can reasonably contribute to the financing of tertiary education. Thus, the formidable policy challenge is that of balancing educational quality against rising enrollments and how to pay for both of them.

The ideal solution lies in a well-managed macroeconomic environment that produces sufficient growth to expand the pool of government revenue so that all economic and social sectors might benefit. A complementary option is for government to encourage further expansion of private provision—in various Asian and Latin American countries, private tertiary enrollments account for 60 percent or more of the total—along with appropriate quality assurance guarantees. An as-yet untested solution is the possibility of developing different and more cost-efficient modes of educational delivery than the traditional model of residential campuses with face-to-face instruction. However, the private-sector institutions are unlikely to produce enough S&E graduates to meet SSA's needs.

Ultimately, the range of policy choices lies between the easy path of *laissez-faire* expansionism, and the more difficult road of strategic quality management. Unfettered expansion is really no solution. It will lead to further declines in educational quality, an overproduction of graduates in relation to the absorptive capacity of the labor market, consequent high unemployment among graduates, and associated risks of political instability, which will increase the difficulties of generating economic growth. Strategically managed expansion will require committed and visionary political leadership capable of coalescing stakeholder agreement concerning key discipline areas for expansion and investment that will provide human resources of the quality required for implementing the national economic development strategy. It will also depend on institutional capacities to forge links with the labor market and to mount productive public-private partnerships around applied research in identified areas of strategic importance. This would need to be complemented by incentives for private provision of education in areas not favored with priority in government funding, and by longer-term efforts to put in place lower-cost delivery models for tertiary education based on combinations of short-cycle courses, nonresidential campuses, computer-assisted instruction, self-paced learning, and distance education. This latter pathway of strategic management seeks to recast tertiary education as an instrument for economic growth, instead of viewing it as a general social entitlement.

Framework for Reform

Africa's recent spurt in economic performance potentially enlarges the resources available for crafting the kinds of tertiary education systems that countries in SSA now require. The danger that growth could slide back to earlier levels if SSA countries do not take measures to sustain it by diversifying and upgrading their industrial bases creates incentives for African policy makers to be far more aggressive in transforming their tertiary education and research systems into one of the principal drivers of national growth. But for tertiary education to contribute to growth, it must itself become more competitive. Given the long lead time it takes to achieve substantial improvements in tertiary system relevance and quality, as well as to build fruitful research institutions, the current window of opportunity is a temporary one. The world will not wait for Africa to catch up.

Specifying the sufficient conditions is one hurdle, but the lesser of two. Translating them into practice will be the harder task to tackle, although examples of relevant successful initiatives can be found in Africa and elsewhere. We divide the sufficient conditions into two task sets that would need to be pursued in tandem. One set addresses the demand for skills and the traversal to a knowledge environment. The other seeks to relieve constraints within tertiary education pertaining to the supply of services and their quality, and to the dissemination of knowledge.

Demand-side Reforms

Demand-side policies seek to maximize the absorption of skilled workers into adequately paid jobs. In addition to interventions contributing to macroeconomic stability and a favorable business climate, productivity-led growth supported by the development of knowledge and skills would be advanced through three types of demand-side interventions. They are:

- incentives for knowledge-intensive industries, both domestic and foreign, and the creation of science parks in the vicinity of leading universities. Regional coordination would help to achieve a critical mass of skills and a desirable scale of market opportunities.
- seed capital for high-tech start-ups. This could be coupled with financial incentives for R&D by public and private firms, institutional and fiscal measures that encourage the provision of such financing, and stronger support for research by public and private research entities. Again, regional coordination and a pooling of resources can make it easier to achieve an optimal scale for research institutes, specialization in research, and a division of labor among countries.
- public-private mechanisms for internships to place tertiary education graduates in firms. This would encourage skill absorption and the transfer of knowledge, particularly to small and medium enterprises. This could be combined with incentive schemes inducing tertiary institutions and firms to enter into collaborative research, design, testing, or product development.

In other words, a tertiary education-supported growth strategy that seeks to raise the quality and volume of skills and knowledge must be buttressed by policies acting on demand for such skills. These policies would ensure an adequate return to skills and induce firms to climb the technology value chain. They could also moderate the brain drain and even create the conditions for a brain gain.

Supply-side Reforms

To fulfill the supply-side conditions, governments need to pursue six tasks. They are to:

- encourage a diverse mix of institutions—private, public, and specialized ones catering to specific segments of industrial needs or the student population.
- strengthen the governance and autonomy of tertiary institutions and stimulate competition among them on a national and even regional basis.
- subject all tertiary institutions to quality-based accreditation requirements, monitoring, and performance assessment.
- take urgent measures to offset the impending retirement of a large fraction of faculty members in public institutions and to simultaneously begin augmenting the supply of instructors, as well as bolstering their caliber, through better pay scales and other professional incentives. This needs to be complemented by an overhaul of pedagogic practices, curricula, and access to libraries, laboratories, and IT facilities.
- foster applied research in a few strategic areas within flagship universities. This could involve providing incentives for tertiary institutions and firms to collaborate in garnering technological capability, and setting up institutions for disseminating and commercializing the fruits of research.
- ensure that reforms, which will be costly to introduce and will need years to reach fruition, are consistently supported by funding from public budgetary sources. But public funding alone will not be sufficient, and consequently must be supplemented from other sources, e.g. tuition fees, income-producing activities, private donations, competitive grants, royalties etc. In other words, a comprehensive financing plan with strong incentives for reform is always the cornerstone of a transformed tertiary education system.

The name of the game now is knowledge-intensive development. It calls for a new outlook—one that is more strategic and nationally integrated—on the nature of the contribution that education can make to industrialization, to exports, to the building of a more resilient economy, and to confronting the twenty-first century challenges posed by climate change, AIDS, food security, energy supply, and more. It calls also for a reappraisal of past empirical findings on the relationship between education and growth in response to changed circumstances. In particular, it points to a rebalancing of the relative attention given to primary, secondary, and tertiary education in light of where countries are with respect to their primary education goals, the state of tertiary education, and the anticipated role that knowledge and skills are expected to have in their future growth. And all of this must be incorporated into a new understanding of the role and mission of tertiary education within a global knowledge economy. This new outlook, together with the policy interventions it implies, comprise a pathway to the vital skills and increased knowledge that African economies are certain to require if they are to increase their competitiveness and thereby sustain their recent growth.

Note

1. Tertiary-level education comprises all post-secondary forms of education, including universities, technical institutes, teaching colleges, open universities, and other programs that lead to the award of academic diplomas or degrees.

CHAPTER 1

Introduction and Context

All countries face developmental challenges. Each of these challenges holds implications for that country's human resource development strategy. Because it is not possible to build a country on basic education alone, secondary and tertiary education—which produce higher-level skills and knowledge—necessarily comprise important elements of any country's approach to development. The arrival of a globally competitive knowledge-driven economy, however, has further underscored the importance of these national capacities for generating social, economic, and political progress.

For nearly two decades, international development assistance has, with few exceptions (see Autor, Levy, and Murnane 2001),[1] viewed the role of postbasic education in Sub-Saharan Africa (SSA) with a blind eye.[2] Pushed by conditionalities and pulled by matching fund requirements, African governments have reluctantly followed suit. In fact, funding priorities—poverty alleviation and millennium development goals—were not wrong, but they were pursued without much attention to associated needs for highly skilled professionals to implement them effectively. As a consequence, official development assistance to postsecondary education in Africa averaged just US$110 million a year between 1990 and 1999, before rising to an average US$515 million a year during the 2000 to 2005 period.[3]

World Bank investments in education reflected this trend, as the Bank often played an important leadership role in focusing international attention on the poorest of the poor in Africa and elsewhere. As a result, its financing for tertiary education on the continent, which had averaged US$ 103 million annually from FY90-FY94, declined to US$ 30.8 million per year from FY95-FY99, and then rose modestly to US$ 36.6 million per year between FY00 and FY04—in sharp contrast to the positive trends in funding for primary and secondary education. In recent years, Bank funding for tertiary education has continued to rise, but the average of $83.9 million between FY05 to 08, still remains below the levels at the start of the 1990s (see Figure 1). Not surprisingly, the deep decline in Bank funding for tertiary education, particularly for a decade between 1994 and 2004, led many in Africa's education community to conclude that the World Bank was an active opponent of tertiary education.

Figure 1.1   New Commitments for Education by Sub-Sector FY1990–2008

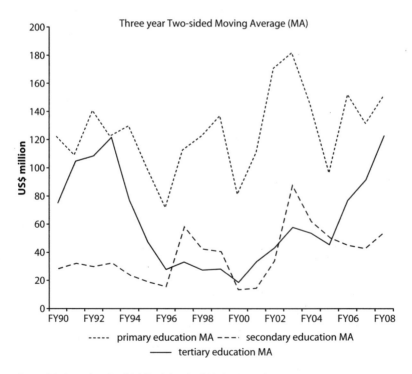

Source: Calculations based on World Bank data. See Table 2 in Appendix A.

In reality, the reasons for this trend in Bank financing went far beyond a simple matter of advocacy for or opposition to a particular subsector of education. In the first comprehensive analysis of educational development in Sub-Saharan Africa, the World Bank (1988) identified the main educational challenges for the continent as the overall stagnation of enrollments and erosion of quality. The report recommended that each country develop an internally coherent set of educational policies that mixed actions of adjustment, revitalization, and selective expansion within each level of education. But economic stagnation prevalent during this period constrained government capacities to finance education reforms and heightened the importance of making carefully considered investment decisions. Growth, social equity, and cost-benefit analysis offered compelling arguments for concentrating investments in basic education. At the same time, the report viewed tertiary education as particularly problematic. It noted that most countries had largely completed the educational task of producing civil servants for their post-independence administrations, and that tertiary education systems were saddled with four weaknesses. First, they were producing relatively too many graduates from programs of dubious quality and relevance, and were generating too little knowledge and direct development support. Second, the quality of these outputs showed unmistakable signs in many countries of having deteriorated so much that the fundamental effectiveness of the institutions was called into question. Third, the costs of higher education were needlessly high, in part due to the widespread practice of providing students with free meals, accommodations, and other social services. Fourth, the pattern of financing for tertiary education was socially inequitable and economically inefficient (World Bank 1988). Moreover, political environments on the continent during the 1990s were less than conducive to tackling the substantial tertiary education reforms necessary to come to grips with these weaknesses. Nations lacked champions of restructuring, strong academic staff unions and student associations opposed reform, and the political pressures on fledgling democracies to expand tertiary education were very strong. All of these factors increased the risks for Bank investments in tertiary education, and steered its funding toward other well-justified and less contentious activities within the education sector (see Table 1.1).

The dawn of the new millennium found these country conditions to be in flux. On the one hand, SSA primary enrollment rates had been raised from 72 percent in 1991 to 80 percent in 1999, and strong donor-government coalitions were in place to oversee the sector's continued

Table 1.1 World Bank Financing for Education in Sub-Saharan Africa, FY1990–FY2008
(US$ millions)

Menu	IBRD and IDA New Commitments (millions of current US$)																		
Sub-sector	FY90	FY91	FY92	FY93	FY94	FY95	FY96	FY97	FY98	FY99	FY00	FY01	FY02	FY03	FY04	FY05	FY06	FY07	FY08
Adult lit/non-formal education	–	2.44	9.22	–	–	–	10.21	–	–	30.45	6.07	–	13.52	0.69	4.63	–	0.72	18.50	–
Gen education sector	57.96	9.36	0.86	2.55	18.02	18.05	36.78	56.50	27.38	10.95	92.90	89.22	128.28	128.91	79.89	174.77	173.46	131.40	190
Pre-primary education	–	–	–	8.03	–	–	–	8.34	–	0.42	–	9.20	–	–	–	–	–	–	7
Primary education	90.74	153.25	82.71	184.35	99.42	104.46	95.45	15.39	226.11	126.47	57.29	59.94	214.18	237.94	91.80	106.11	90.56	257.90	45
Secondary education	38.65	18.54	40.21	32.19	25.74	12.28	–	18.98	98.17	10.85	13.65	14.40	–	53.92	124.20	11.19	18.26	106.60	4
Tertiary education	119.72	30.67	163.75	131.04	69.94	30.20	41.76	11.59	46.00	24.68	13.95	17.02	69.48	–	45.93	61.16	29.07	140.10	105
Vocational training	3.13	6.66	27.36	6.25	55.37	10.04	10.45	4.41	2.37	4.94	5.92	19.75	47.15	2.12	16.46	15.80	27.20	51.50	22
Total Africa Region	**310.20**	**220.93**	**324.11**	**364.42**	**268.48**	**175.02**	**194.64**	**115.21**	**400.03**	**208.76**	**189.77**	**209.53**	**472.61**	**423.58**	**362.91**	**369.02**	**339.26**	**707.00**	**373**

Source: EDU Lending Website Calculation

Note: The general education sector includes more than one sub-sector. About 50% of financing under "general education" is for primary education.

development (UNESCO 2007).[4] On the other hand, economic growth rates were improving, and rates of return to investments in tertiary education appeared to be rising in response to the demands for higher-level skills and increased knowledge management. In addition, engagement with tertiary education transformation rippled out across the continent from South Africa, where an intensive process of postapartheid policy analysis and consensus building profoundly reshaped that nation's tertiary education system. As a result, many of the earlier reservations to the Bank's engagement with tertiary education in Africa faded from prominence because of achievement and change, even as compelling new justifications for tertiary education development pushed to the fore.

Against this backdrop of changed circumstances, the World Bank recognizes the need to update its understanding of tertiary education in Africa, define its current views on this matter, and offer technical support on this topic to its collaborating governments and development partners. The present study seeks to fulfill this purpose. It provides a justification for African and donor investments in tertiary education within the context of a globally competitive knowledge economy, and suggests likely focus areas for this financing. But it does not pretend to offer a comprehensive assessment of tertiary education in Africa, an overall agenda for its reform, or a new policy statement by the Bank itself. Rather, the study strives to share contemporary insights and experience regarding the relationship between human resource development and economic growth. Its main audience includes the staffs of African governments, development partner agencies, African tertiary education systems, and the World Bank, who have been given responsibilities for nurturing human resource development in Sub-Saharan Africa and for ensuring that investments in tertiary education make a strategic and durable contribution to the growth and competitiveness of Africa's economies.

Context

The greatest challenge for development professionals is how to improve the economic performance of SSA and sustain it. Many solutions have been proposed, but when applied through policies, they have generally proven to be ineffective. However, past and ongoing efforts have enlarged our understanding of the constraints on economic growth, in particular, constraints that check labor productivity, limit export diversification, and reduce innovation. These constraints have a number of causes, among which the volume and quality of tertiary education and research are becoming increasingly prominent as the links between technology and growth strengthen in developed and developing economies alike.

This study examines the relationship between economic growth and education in SSA, focusing primarily, but by no means exclusively, on seven countries—Ghana, Kenya, Mauritius, Nigeria, South Africa, Tanzania, and Uganda. The study provides an overview of growth performance and its key drivers. It defines some of the principal economic challenges confronting SSA and the available options for promoting growth, especially through a diversification of economic activities and exports, and a deepening of technological capabilities. Such diversification is predicated on the success of measures to raise the standards of tertiary education and research, and to multiply the links between tertiary institutions and the business sectors. The study briefly assesses the current performance of tertiary education and its contribution to business activities, and based on this, it delineates a number of policy actions that could help raise its quality and contribute to technology-led development in Africa.

The study draws upon 16 separate background papers, including a survey of university-industry linkages in the selected countries, and an empirical examination of the changing pattern of exports from SSA countries. The information derived from these papers is complemented by various rankings of competitiveness, and buttressed by the results derived from other relevant research. The study proposes a strategy for enhancing the performance of countries in SSA that uses reforms in tertiary education as the fulcrum. Almost no one now doubts that modern economic growth anywhere in the world is becoming more, rather than less, skill intensive, and is requiring increasingly higher levels of education, technical competence, and computer literacy.[5]

Although earlier studies cast doubt on the contribution of human capital to growth (Bils and Klenow 2000; Pritchett 2001), more recent research suggests that growth will falter if the supply of human capital is insufficient (see Cohen and Soto 2007; Lutz, Cuaresma, and Sanderson 2008).[6] A related and intuitively appealing finding is that the quality of education has a stronger bearing on growth outcomes than just the volume of skills produced, after countries have passed a certain threshold level of literacy and an average per-capita level of education. Hanushek and Woessmann (2007) estimate that "the quality of education independently affects economic outcomes even after allowing for other factors . . . quality may come from formal schools, from parents, or from other influences on students. But a more skilled population—almost certainly including both a broadly educated population and a cadre of top

performers— results in stronger economic performance for nations."
According to Bloom, Canning, and Chan (2006b), Sub-Saharan Africa's
production level is 23 percent below its production possibility frontier
because of a shortfall in human capital. By raising the stock of tertiary
education by one year, these economies could raise their growth by 0.24
percentage points (from an increase in factor inputs), and by an additional 0.39 percentage points through an increase in productivity. While
growth based on factor inputs would diminish after the first year if there
is no subsequent increase, higher productivity would be sustained until it
converges to the global frontier, and would eventually increase the per-
capita gross domestic product (GDP) of African countries by 12 percent.

Past research found that social rates of return to tertiary education
were lower than those for primary and secondary education.
Psacharopoulos and Patrinos (2004) estimated that the worldwide average social rate of return to tertiary education was 10.8 percent, whereas
the worldwide average return to primary education was 18.9 percent.[7]
By comparison, the private rate of return to higher education was 19 percent, against 26.6 percent for primary education.[8] However, other
research shows that private returns to higher education can be greater
than to primary and secondary education. This is seen mainly in developing countries, where high-level skills are relatively scarce (see table 1.2).

Furthermore, in recent years, the returns to higher education have been
increasing. Globally, the return to higher education has increased 1.7 percentage points in the last 15 years, whereas the return to primary education
has decreased by 2.0 percentage points (Psacharopoulos 2006). Results

Table 1.2   Private Returns to Primary vs. Tertiary Education

	Private Returns to		
Country/Region	Primary education	Tertiary education	Authors
World	26.6%	19.0%	Psacharopoulos and Patrinos 2004
Papua New Guinea	6.0%	9.2%	Gibson and Fatai 2006
Philippines	9–10%	17.0%	Schady 2003
India	2.4%	10.3%	Dutta 2006
Kenya	7.7%	25.1%	Kimenyi, Mwabu, and Manda 2006
Nigeria	2–3%	10–15%	Aromolaran 2006
Ethiopia	25.0%	27.0%	World Bank 2003

Source: Authors.

from a study by the organisation for Economic Co-operation and Development (OECD) also point to a slight upward trend in returns to tertiary education among OECD countries (Boarini and Strauss 2007).[9] The return to tertiary education has increased in India from 9 percent in 1983 to 10.3 percent in 1999 (Dutta 2006). Similarly, returns to higher education in some of the Sub-Saharan countries are increasing (Schultz 2004). Moreover, the relative wages of tertiary-educated workers have been rising in Latin America, despite a large increase in tertiary education enrollment. This suggests that the demand for skilled workers has strengthened, mainly because of technology transfer and trade reforms, which have intensified competitive pressures (de Ferranti and others 2003).[10] A number of studies have shown that when an economy is faced with changes, be it from the introduction of new technologies such as the Green Revolution, transition to a market economy, or the liberalization of an economy, education plays a key role in facilitating such changes, and the more educated economies are the ones that drive the process and gain the most (Dutta 2006; Foster and Rosenzweig 1996; Yang 2005). Research on the perceived rates of return to education supports the above findings. For example, the ex-ante rates of return (calculated from secondary school students prior to graduation) from higher education in Cyprus were perceived to be 9.4 percent in 2003–04, compared to 6.7 percent in 1993–04, reflecting the higher demand for university graduates. Part of this came from Cyprus's expected accession to the European Union, which took place in 2004, enlarging economic opportunities (Menon 2008). Thus, both the ex-post analysis (in much of empirical literature) and the ex-ante analysis point to the importance of tertiary education and rising rates of return to higher education.[11,12]

Economic Status and Prospects

Over a 20-year period extending from the mid–1970s up to the mid–1990s, per-capita GDP growth in SSA was either zero or negative (Artadi and Sala-i-Martin 2003). Among developing regions, SSA registered the weakest economic performance (Ndulu and others 2007).[13] Starting in the latter part of the 1990s, growth began to strengthen. Aggregate GDP growth averaged 2.3 percent during 1995–2000. Since 2001 it has accelerated further and averaged almost 6 percent per annum through 2007–08 (Economist Intelligence Unit 2006a; 2006b), although growth of per-capita GDP is a little over 2 percent because population growth in SSA remains high.[14] A few countries are expanding their GDP growth much faster because they are starting from a low base and are exporters of petroleum or mineral products, with Angola, Equatorial Guinea, Mauritania, and Sudan being at the forefront.[15] Table 1.3 presents some of the key indicators for the seven countries in our sample for 1990 and 2006. Except for Mauritius, which experienced a 56 percent growth in per-capita GDP in constant 2000 dollars, in the other countries,

Table 1.3   Growth and Sectoral Indicators

Country/Region	Indicators	1990	2006
Ghana	GDP growth (annual %)	3.3	6.2
	GDP per capita (constant 2000 US$)	211.0	299.6
	Manufacturing, value added (% of GDP)	9.8	7.6
	Services, etc., value added (% of GDP)	38.4	41.1
Kenya	GDP growth (annual %)	4.2	5.7
	GDP per capita (constant 2000 US$)	450.6	455.8
	Manufacturing, value added (% of GDP)	11.7	12.1
	Services, etc., value added (% of GDP)	51.4	54.8
Mauritius	GDP growth (annual %)	5.8	3.5
	GDP per capita (constant 2000 US$)	2,532.1	4,522.3
	Manufacturing, value added (% of GDP)	24.7	19.1
	Services, etc., value added (% of GDP)	53.8	67.6
Nigeria	GDP growth (annual %)	8.2	5.9
	GDP per capita (constant 2000 US$)	357.5	439.0
	Manufacturing, value added (% of GDP)	5.5	..
	Services, etc., value added (% of GDP)	25.9	19.4
South Africa	GDP growth (annual %)	−0.3	5.0
	GDP per capita (constant 2000 US$)	3,151.8	3,562.1
	Manufacturing, value added (% of GDP)	23.6	18.2
	Services, etc., value added (% of GDP)	55.3	67.0
Tanzania	GDP growth (annual %)	7.0	5.9
	GDP per capita (constant 2000 US$)	259.3	334.6
	Manufacturing, value added (% of GDP)	9.3	6.9
	Services, etc., value added (% of GDP)	36.4	37.3
Uganda	GDP growth (annual %)	6.5	5.3
	GDP per capita (constant 2000 US$)	173.3	274.3
	Manufacturing, value added (% of GDP)	5.7	8.6
	Services, etc., value added (% of GDP)	32.4	43.7
Sub-Saharan Africa	GDP growth (annual %)	1.1	5.6
	GDP per capita (constant 2000 US$)	529.0	583.4
	Manufacturing, value added (% of GDP)	16.6	14.4
	Services, etc., value added (% of GDP)	46.8	52.3
East Asia & Pacific	GDP growth (annual %)	5.5	9.4
	GDP per capita (constant 2000 US$)	481.2	1,472.6
	Manufacturing, value added (% of GDP)	29.8	30.8
	Services, etc., value added (% of GDP)	35.1	42.4

Source: World Development Indicators (2007).

it increased much less. Two countries raised their share of manufacturing in GDP—Kenya from 11.7 percent to 12.1 percent, and Uganda from 5.7 percent to 8.6 percent. All others saw their shares decline, a significant and worrisome trend.

The principal sources of the economic revival since the beginning of the decade are the higher prices of energy and raw materials, coupled with a rise in the volumes traded. They are reinforced by an increase in the exports of light manufactures and farm products, and greater investment in housing, commercial real estate, and infrastructure, which have been buoyed by aid and remittances. The former are much larger than the latter. For SSA, remittances amount to just 2.5 percent of GDP, compared to an average of 5 percent for other developing countries.[16,17] For the countries in our sample, they are insignificant for Kenya, Mauritius, South Africa, and Tanzania. They are slightly higher in Ghana (0.9 percent) and highest in Uganda (9.7 percent) (see table 1.4).

The economic revival has not, however, changed the fundamentals. The sources of long-term growth are weak, and African countries continue to lag behind others in terms of exports, investment, industrial output, economic rankings, doing business indicators, and knowledge indicators. SSA's share of global industrial output fell from 0.79 in 1990 to 0.74 in 2002. If South Africa is excluded, the share in 2002 was 0.25 percent (UNIDO 2004). Although the share of developing countries in manufacturing value added (MVA) globally rose from 17 percent in 1990 to 24 percent in 2001, that of SSA countries declined, and they lost ground in all subsectors except textiles, apparel, leather, footwear, and basic metals, which have benefited from rising domestic demand. The low share of manufacturing value added is reflected in table 1.3. Between 2001 and 2005, SSA's share of MVA shrank even further despite strengthening growth performance, because growth of manufacturing in other industrializing countries also accelerated. Some diversification of manufactured and agricultural exports has occurred (e.g. a large increase in the export of cut flowers from Ethiopia), but it is fairly modest. SSA's portion of world trade rose between 2003 and 2005, but only fractionally—from 2.5 percent to 2.9 percent. This is approximately one–third of its share in the middle of the twentieth century, as is apparent from table 1.5, where export/GDP ratios in the seven countries are generally well-below those of East Asian countries, Mauritius being an exception. Nigeria's relatively high percentage reflects the scale of its oil exports. Moreover, Africa's dependence on primary products remains undiminished. Over three-quarters of all exports are comprised of primary commodities (86 percent purchased by Asia), and

Table 1.4   Remittances and Foreign Assistance
(Percent of GDP)

Country	Indicators	2001	2005
Ghana	Workers' remittances, receipts (BoP, current US$)	0.9%	0.9%
	Official development assistance and official aid	12.1%	10.4%
	Aid (% of gross capital formation)	45.3%	36.0%
Kenya	Workers' remittances, receipts (BoP, current US$)	0.0%	1.0%
	Official development assistance and official aid	3.5%	4.0%
	Aid (% of gross capital formation)	18.4%	24.4%
Mauritius	Workers' remittances, receipts (BoP, current US$)	0.0%	–
	Official development assistance and official aid	0.2%	0.5%
	Aid (% of gross capital formation)	2.0%	2.2%
Nigeria	Workers' remittances, receipts (BoP, current US$)	2.4%	3.4%
	Official development assistance and official aid	0.4%	6.6%
	Aid (% of gross capital formation)	1.5%	31.2%
South Africa	Workers' remittances, receipts (BoP, current US$)	0.0%	–
	Official development assistance and official aid	0.4%	0.3%
	Aid (% of gross capital formation)	2.4%	1.6%
Tanzania	Workers' remittances, receipts (BoP, current US$)	0.1%	0.1%
	Official development assistance and official aid	0.1%	12.0%
	Aid (% of gross capital formation)	79.4%	65.8%
Uganda	Workers' remittances, receipts (BoP, current US$)	6.0%	9.7% [a]
	Official development assistance and official aid	14.0%	13.7%
	Aid (% of gross capital formation)	74.9%	64.8%

Source: World Development Indicators (2006).
a. Data is from 2000.
b. BoP = Balance of payments.

two-thirds of export revenues are derived from petroleum alone (Broadman 2007). The shares of engineering, food, and garment exports are still relatively low, except for Mauritius (see table 1.6).[18] Higher prices of oil and other primary commodities accounted for much of the increase

Table 1.5   Exports of Goods and Services
(Percent of GDP)

Country/Region	1990	2006
Ghana	16.9%	39.2%
Kenya	25.7%	24.3%
Mauritius	64.2%	59.7%
Nigeria	43.4%	53.4%[a]
South Africa	24.2%	29.1%
Tanzania	12.6%	24.3%
Uganda	7.2%	13.8%
Sub-Saharan Africa	27.0%	32.1%
East Asia & Pacific	24.0%	43.8%

Source: World Development Indicators (2006).
a. Data is from 2005.

Table 1.6   Share of Engineering, Food, and Garment Exports in Selected Countries, 2001–06

Country	Avg. share of engineering exports (2001–06)	Avg. share of processed food exports (2001–06)	Avg. share of garment exports (2001–06)	Avg. share of all three category's exports (2001–06)
Botswana	1.13	0.67	2.45	4.31
Ghana	0.50	8.62	0.07	9.54
Kenya	1.32	8.91	0.38	10.57
Mauritius	2.62	23.28	47.49	73.18
South Africa	8.81	4.19	0.73	13.73

Source: World Development Indicators (2007).

in export earnings during 2005.[19] Growth in volume, however, at 5.2 percent, was a little less than the global trade growth rate of 6 percent (Economist Intelligence Unit 2007a).

Investment and domestic savings rates are an additional source of weakness. Investment rates in the early 1960s averaged between 7 percent and 8 percent of GDP, rising to a high point of about 13 percent during 1975–80, before falling back to about 7.5 percent during 1990–95. Starting in the second half of the 1990s, they have risen slowly and are currently close to 10 percent (Artadi and Sala-i-Martin 2003). The cause of low investment in SSA, which constrains growth, is apparently not a consequence of inadequate financing, but more closely related to risk perception on the part of investors (Bigsten and others 1999; Fafchamps and Oostendorp 2002; Gunning and Mengistae 2001). For the seven countries in our sample, savings rates were in the 20 percent range in 2005 for Kenya, Mauritius, and South Africa. They were half that level in Tanzania, Uganda, and Ghana, but much higher in Nigeria because of oil exports (see figure 1.2). However, investment in the 18 percent to 25 percent range is still significantly lower than in East Asian countries during their earlier stage of industrialization in the 1970s and 1980s, and well below that of China and India today (Ndulu and others 2007).

The indicators of competitiveness are equally troubling.[20] Of the seven countries in our sample—which include some of the most promising economies in the region—all but South Africa and Mauritius register poor scores on five indexes (see table 1.7). South Africa is consistently the highest ranked among the seven countries on all of the indexes, but it is behind Malaysia on the Growth Competitiveness Index (GCI), the Knowledge for Development (K4D), the Doing Business, and the United Nations Industrial Development Organization (UNIDO) indexes. It is only ahead on the country rankings because of its size. Kenya, Uganda, South Africa, Nigeria, and Ghana have experienced a decline in the GCI and the UNIDO rankings, and have either stayed constant or fallen

Figure 1.2   Savings and Investment, 1990–2006
(% of GDP)

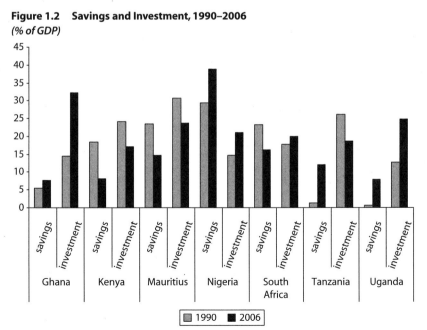

Source: World Development Indicators (2006).
Note: Data for Nigeria are from 2005.

Table 1.7 Competitiveness of SSA Countries (Various Rankings)

Country	Global Competitiveness Index (125 countries)			Knowledge for Development Index (K4D) (131 countries)			Doing business (175 countries)			UNIDO (87 countries)			Global economic prospect country ranking (130 countries)		
	2006	1998	Change	Most Recent	1995	Change	2006	2005	Change	1998	1985	Change	2005	1980	Change
Kenya	94	–	–	3.10	2.85	0.25	83	80	–3	62	64	2	73	78	5
Uganda	113	–	–	2.42	2.48	–0.06	107	103	–4	84	80	–4	99	103	4
Tanzania	104	–	–	2.33	2.44	–0.11	142	150	8	80	70	–10	86	65	–21
South Africa	45	42	–3	6.00	6.15	–0.15	29	28	–1	39	32	–7	28	22	–6
Mauritius	55	29	–26	5.08	4.84	0.24	32	32	0	56	47	–9	103	115	12
Nigeria	101	–	–	2.61	2.60	0.01	108	109	1	78	75	–3	49	33	–16
Ghana	–	–	–	2.40	2.54	–0.14	94	102	8	86	76	–10	93	89	–4
Vietnam	77	39	–38	3.74	3.00	0.74	104	98	–6	–	–	–	56	35	–21
Malaysia	26	–	–	6.33	5.86	0.47	25	25	0	22	30	8	38	43	5

Sources: Global Competitiveness Index: http://www.weforum.org/pdf/Global_Competitiveness_Reports/Reports/gcr_2006/gcr2006_summary.pdf. Knowledge for Development Index: http://info.worldbank.org/etools/KAM_page5.asp. Doing business: http://www.doingbusiness.org/ExploreEconomies/?economyif=197 (Doing Business 2007). UNIDO: http://www.unido.org/doc/24397, Industrial Development Report 2002–03 (2003). Global economic prospect: "Managing the Next Wave of Globalization," World Bank 2007.

Note: –not ranked.

behind in the K4D rankings. Tanzania has improved its Doing Business ranking by 8 points between 2005 and 2006. And Kenya, Uganda, and Mauritius have improved their country GDP weighted rankings, although these remain quite low: 73, 99, and 102, within a group of 130 countries.[21]

Although the growth performance since 2001 is encouraging, past experience warns that were the commodity boom to deflate, the growth rates of the fortunate SSA countries would most likely slide back to the levels achieved in the first half of the 1990s.[22] A persistence of high energy prices and higher food prices severely affect energy- and grain-importing countries such as Eritrea, and would most likely dampen the growth performance of the continent as a whole. Cross-country experiences of developing economies indicate that the likelihood of maintaining growth in the 5 percent to 7 percent range (even the higher figure would permit a less than 5 percent increase in per-capita GDP) depends on eventually attaining a manufacturing base accounting for 25 percent to 30 percent of GDP and on producer services of a scale comparable to manufacturing. In countries that have achieved such growth rates for long periods, savings and investments have averaged 30 percent to 35 percent or more, and rarely fallen below 25 percent.[23] Both the rising skill intensity of industrial development and the increasing contribution of producer services to growth suggest that technical skills will play a larger role. Nevertheless, especially in the earlier stages of development, capital will remain the principal driver of growth.

Challenges and Options

A far more competitive trading environment, the course of technological change, and the capabilities in manufacturing and services acquired by countries in South and East Asia have drastically curtailed options that might have been within reach of a few African countries 15 years ago (see also Collier 2007). Now only difficult choices remain. These include:

- attempting to make a success of the traditional model of development by enlarging these countries' extremely small share in the international markets for standardized manufacturing industries and agro-industrial products, where the value-added for the producer can be small, competition is intense, and survival depends on fully exploiting the lower costs of land, labor, utilities, and a more relaxed regime of environmental regulations, while becoming a part of global value chains. Diversification into higher-value agricultural or industrial products promising better returns will entail higher-order participation in "buyer-driven" supply chains and networks, in meeting the delivery, reliability, and innovation expectations of the buyers, and satisfying the certification requirements and standards set for higher-value items.[24] Suppliers of specialty coffees and others who have set up wet processing plants and improved the quality of their coffee have been able to meet the requirements and integrate with global supply chains (UNCTAD 2007). The rapidly expanding market for certified organic products offers opportunities that Uganda is beginning to exploit with its fresh fruit, vegetables, and cotton (Raynolds 2004). Unfortunately, meeting organic certification—which entails extensive record-keeping, the careful mapping of holdings, purging the land of synthetic fertilizer, and hand removal of pests—is difficult for the small holder. So also is participation in global food chains in which buyers are keen to push responsibilities onto the shoulders of suppliers (Humphrey and Memedovic 2006). Thus, success in these markets is coming to depend upon the emergence of large suppliers who can deal with certification requirements and the demand for product uniformity, prompt delivery, appropriate packaging, and a steady stream of new products, processed items, and packaging (Raynolds 2004). SSA agricultural producers and agro-processing companies—except those from South Africa—lag far behind in scale, and consequently other countries are snapping up the new market opportunities.[25]

- diversifying into less hotly contested niche markets for low- and medium-tech manufactures or agricultural products, searching out untapped technological possibilities, and innovating in the hope of entering new markets, e.g., in biofuels.
- gaining a foothold in the markets for tradable services and in particular, IT-enabled services, which countries such as Ghana are now attempting.
- moving up the value chain for natural resources by processing more of these domestically, and exploiting backward linkages by building engineering or input supplying industries for the mineral resource extraction sector, as South Africa has done.
- making a start at achieving technological capabilities with a more intensive effort at assimilating available knowledge with the help of patent specialists and new search software (see Arora, Fosfuri, and Gambardella 2001),[26] for example, in higher technology industries that are of greatest relevance for the region, such as agricultural biotechnology,[27] wooden furniture,[28]alternative energy sources,[29] new materials based on indigenous agricultural products, software,[30]

food processing, and others for which the initial cost in terms of capital outlay are not unusually large.

- carefully managing natural resources so as to maximize the returns, whether through the negotiation and monitoring of contracts with multinational corporations that are extracting mineral resources, the application of the most efficient techniques for extraction, or the sustainable management of renewable resources such as forests or game reserves. Environmental issues will become more urgent and much more difficult to address as populations grow and the climate becomes less favorable.

For the SSA region, the urgency of shifting tracks to a different growth path is rendered more acute by:

- impending climate change and its implications for landlocked countries in the interior, but also some coastal ones (*Economist* 2007). Adverse climate trends are virtually a certainty. The only remaining imponderables are the rapidity of onset and its severity. The grassland areas in Eastern and Southern Africa are most likely to be affected by rising temperatures, lower rainfall, and desertification.[31] Water availability and severe climatic extremes will be problems throughout the region. And coastal areas will be affected by inundation, destruction of coral reefs, and loss of coastal fisheries, perhaps more so in West Africa than in the East. The implications for agriculture and the tourist sector will be profound.[32]
- pressures generated by AIDS[33] and other diseases that affect dependency ratios, fertility, labor productivity, primary enrollment, school attendance, number of orphans, nutrition during early childhood, and many other variables.
- tensions arising from the growth of the population and labor force (see figure 1.3), migration to cities, and the share of population under 18 years of age—the so-called "youth bulge" (Cincotta 2005).[34]
- economic vulnerabilities created by the unequal distribution of incomes. Inequality is associated with economic slowdown and greater fragility in the face of external shocks (Johnson, Ostry, and Subramanian 2007).[35] Vulnerabilities also arise from the isolation and high transport costs affecting some of the landlocked countries.[36]
- lags in exploiting new farming technologies, which have constrained productivity and increased vulnerability to pests and weather extremes.[37]

Figure 1.3   Population Growth and Fertility Rates for Selected Countries, 1990 and 2005

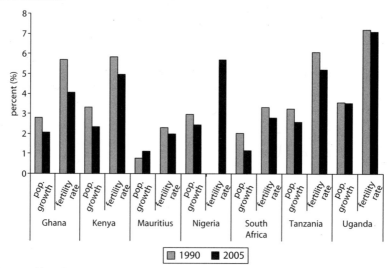

Source: World Development Indicators (2006).
Note: Data on fertility for Nigeria is from 2002.

- problems with planning and implementing projects, and with regulating and maintaining physical infrastructure.[38]
- brain drain and the losses inflicted by the high mortality of the educated because of AIDS, which has worsened the shortage of skills (Ndulu 2004; Ndulu and others 2007).
- an underdeveloped and distorted institutional infrastructure, which is responsible for the unfavorable business climate, technological backwardness, failing tertiary institutions, and chronic social unrest.[39]

Needless to say, except for light manufacturing industries and low-tech agro-processing, many of the other options will depend on the availability of ample supplies of skilled and technical workers, as well as on access to risk capital to finance new starts in higher-technology activities. Initially at least, until financial markets deepen, a substantial portion of this capital may have to come from public sources as is the case throughout East Asia. Johnson, Ostry, and Subramanian (2007) have observed that in certain respects, SSA countries are well-positioned for a growth surge. Many have achieved macroeconomic stability and have liberalized trade. At the same time, economic institutions that impinge on business activity are weak and exchange rates are appreciating. Moreover, only 12 low-income countries have sustained rapid growth for long periods, and in almost all cases, this was because exports of manufactures expanded strongly. As Rodrik (2006) has shown, the poor performance of South Africa, SSA's most advanced economy, can be largely explained by the slow growth of its tradable manufacturing sector.

Barring exceedingly large injections of resources from overseas, gross national investment of 30 percent or more is unlikely for the vast majority of SSA countries, particularly in the resource-poor ones. Thus, the higher rates of growth that SSA countries are seeking will only be achieved through gains in the efficiency of resource use and in total factor productivity derived from advances in technology. Once growth rates ascend to a higher plane, savings and investment are likely to climb, as they have in India, for instance, and could reach East Asian levels. But this is bound to be a slow process as per-capita incomes rise, confidence in the future strengthens, capital flight (which has diverted 40 percent of the region's wealth overseas) is curtailed or reversed, and debilitating sociopolitical problems responsible for violence and unrest are attenuated (Bates, Coatsworth, and Williamson 2006; Collier 2007; Freeman and Lindauer 1999; Ndulu and others 2007). In the meantime, accelerating growth, viewed from the perspective of supply, requires:

- sharp gains in allocative efficiency, mediated by public agencies, the financial system,[40] and the business sector;
- a substantial increase in the efficiency with which capital assets (infrastructure and industrial) are utilized, and sustained efforts are made to maintain these assets;[41]
- a steady improvement in the capacity to search for and assimilate relevant technology, to make incremental advances, and to harness technology for a variety of purposes—producing tradables, improving public health, and conserving energy and water being some of them;[42] and
- an accumulation of managerial and organizational skills and experience, not only to support industrialization and international economic relations, but also to cope with the trends toward decentralization in several dimensions, and of urbanization. Fiscal and administrative decentralization that is ongoing in many African countries, and the growth of urban centers, will require a deepening of soft skills.[43] Where these have remained weak, countries are confronting severe fiscal pressures and urban crises that can gravely hamper, if not cripple, development.

All these are predicated on an increase in the ratio of skilled and technical workers to capital, at a relatively earlier stage of development. As Theodore W. Schultz (1975) pointed out in a famous paper over 30 years ago, trained workers and professionals not only provide technical knowledge and promote innovation, they also serve as allocators of resources, and as coordinators and equilibrators who can perceive and exploit technological possibilities. Where resources are invested, the assessment of risks, the technologies employed, the organization of production, the upgrading and maintenance of assets, the investment in Research and Development (R&D), the incentive to innovate, and the commercialization of new technologies depend on choices made by decision makers operating in public and private capacities. The quality of these myriad decisions is as significant for the eventual outcomes as the direct input of human capital in the production process. These allocative and risk-managing functions, the making of multiple trade-offs, and the communicating and cooperating with many different parties to improve the quality of decisions are vital complements to the activity of innovation. Together they help enlarge the contribution of knowledge to economic performance.

The United States was able to raise its "speed limit" of growth to between 3 percent and 4 percent from 1995–2005 when gross investment averaged 20 percent and net investment was as low as 7.5 percent, because it had the combination of entrepreneurial, managerial, and technical skills to exploit the opportunities presented by the IT revolution (Jorgenson and Stiroh 2000; Nordhaus 2001; Solow 2001).[44] The aggregate indicators of growth and total factor productivity are mirrored by industry-level indicators of labor productivity, which consistently show that the United States is more productive in virtually every sector than any other country. The United States does not lead other countries with respect to capital/labor ratios;[45] however, it does lead in terms of the volume of innovation and more important—for example in IT—in the assimilation and commercialization of innovations. Between 1973 and 1990, productivity growth in SSA was negative, declining 1.16 percentage points per annum. Since then, some improvement is discernible, but clearly the potential remains for further gains as the scope for technology catch-up and spillovers is immense (Ndulu and others 2007).

Brain Drain: How Serious?

Improving the quality of human capital and how it is deployed offer an alternative route to faster growth in SSA,[46] where physical capital is relatively scarce and likely to remain so for some time. Policy makers in

African countries worry that many of those who receive expensive tertiary-level training, whether at home or in foreign countries, will emigrate or not return once their studies are completed. This has been an issue that many parts of SSA have had to wrestle with for some time, and it has been a concern for other countries, developing and developed. The emigration of skilled people particularly affects smaller countries and middle-income countries more than low-income ones (Docquier and Marfouk 2005). For example, one-third of the Caribbean workforce with secondary and tertiary education has emigrated, and almost two-thirds from Jamaica and Haiti (Lowell B. Lindsay 2003). High levels of emigration affect, among others, the Hong Kong (China), United Kingdom, and Vietnam. In the 1960s and 1970s, a fifth of Taiwanese students went abroad to study and few returned. Over a 30-year period, perhaps 100,000 left (O'Neil 2003). In the case of the worst affected SSA countries, brain drain, compounded by losses from HIV/AIDS,[47] has also increased the dependence on foreign experts, as many as 100,000 of whom work in the region at an annual cost of US$4 billion (Ndulu and others 2007). In the face of these losses, it is desirable to have a better sense of its seriousness, and clarity as to what can be done about it.

First, although the statistics are less than reliable, the outflow of skilled and technical workers might not be unmanageable for many of the countries. Even the highest estimate of emigration by physicians, who are among those most likely to depart, is only 28 percent, and the lowest estimate is 9 percent.[48] Far fewer engineers and technicians are likely to emigrate. These percentages are high but comparable to those experienced by East and South Asian countries from the 1960s through the 1990s. Second, most of the emigration (as of 2000) is from countries that had experienced a difficult spell, e.g., Eritrea, Liberia, Mozambique, Sierra Leone, and Somalia, but large numbers of the skilled have also left Ghana and Mauritius. Some of this emigration is intraregional. In fact, 63 percent of all migrants (and not just the skilled) stayed in SSA, and only a quarter went to OECD countries. The former are more likely to return (World Bank 2008e). Third, an increasing number of Africans leaving for overseas training now head to China. Currently, there are over 2,000 students from SSA enrolled in Science and Engineering courses in China, and the numbers are rising very rapidly. A relatively high percentage of these are likely to return to their home countries.

There is, of course, the fourth factor, which is the volume of remittances that migrants send back each year. The approximately 16 million migrants from SSA countries remitted US$22 billion in 2006, which is a notable injection of resources, especially for smaller countries such as Burkina Faso, Burundi, Guinea-Bissau, Lesotho, and Liberia (IFAD 2008). Moreover, as China, India, and Korea have discovered, the diaspora can serve as a "knowledge bank" and a source of foreign investment and networking relationships that can assist flows of trade.

Some brain drain is inevitable[49] and needs to be factored into the calculations of governments. When it becomes "excessive," it clearly depletes countries of some of their most valuable resources. However, countries cannot, as Benno Ndulu notes, "contain the problem of brain drain by erecting hurdles to contain emigration.... Talent will flee from where it finds no gainful use. Expanding opportunities for gainful and well-remunerated engagement is part of a lasting solution to the brain drain problem. . . . Better skills lead to higher growth, and in turn higher growth leads to an increased demand for skills" (Ndulu and others 2007). SSA countries need to redouble their efforts at building the required stock of higher-level human capital to offset the brain drain, and under conditions of globalization, to pursue a risky but more attractive strategy that emphasizes skill intensity and the quality of skills so as to stimulate innovation, to promote diversification of products and services, and to maximize returns from capital assets through more efficient allocation and management.

Economic Diversification

In order to diversify the export basket and reap growth benefits, countries need to "discover" new export goods (Rodrik 2007). The pattern of discovery varies widely among regions, and the process of accelerating "good" discoveries is poorly understood.[50] But one plausible hypothesis is that the discovery of new export possibilities is the combined outcome of entrepreneurship and skills, as well as production capability and a policy-induced investment climate that make it possible to respond quickly to perceived opportunities.[51] SSA lags because of persisting gaps in these areas. When the value of new exports is measured as the weighted average of per-capita income of exporting countries,[52] the new discoveries in East Asia in 2004 totaled US$4 billion, compared to US$3 million in Latin America and the Caribbean. The mean value of a new discovery from 2000 to 2005 in East Asia was US$50,000; it was US$12,000 in Latin America and US$4,000 in SSA (Chandra, Boccardo, and Osorio 2007). On average, a strong and positive relationship is found between secondary and tertiary skills and export competitiveness levels in developing countries (see figures 1.4 and 1.5). However, for about the same level of tertiary

Figure 1.4   Export Sophistication and Competitiveness (EXPY) and Level of Higher Education (Percent of the Labor Force that has Completed Higher Education)

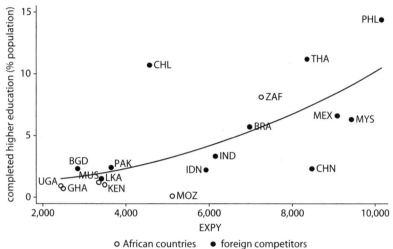

o African countries   ● foreign competitors

Source: Education corresponds to year 1999 from Barro and Lee (2000) estimates. EXPY was calculated using UN Comtrade SITC Rev. 2–4 digits for 2000–2004.
Notes: BRA-Brazil; BGD-Bangladesh; CHL-Chile; CHN-China; GHA-Ghana; IND-India; IDN-Indonesia; KEN-Kenya; LKA-Sri Lanka; MEX-Mexico; MOZ-Mozambique; MUS-Mauritius; MYS-Malaysia; PAK-Pakistan; PHL-Philippines; THA-Thailand; UGA-Uganda; ZAF-South Africa.

education, Ghana, Kenya, and Uganda have significantly lower levels of export sophistication and competitiveness (measured by the Rodrik-Hausmann score of export sophistication and competitiveness, known as the EXPY index) than China, India, and Indonesia. This suggests that other factors may be responsible for the relatively slow rate of discovery by SSA countries.

Some countries, such as Ethiopia, Kenya, Tanzania, and Uganda, have been able to "discover" new export goods. A larger proportion of their exports are now comprised of high-value primary products, resource-based products, and some light manufactures (see Figure 1.6).[53] Many countries were able to reduce their reliance on a few key export products, although the dependence on their top five products is still rather high. Tanzania has made good progress toward diversifying its export portfolio. However, the increase in export sophistication has been relatively modest (see table 1.8). For Ghana and Mauritius, export sophistication actually declined between 1985 and 2004.

East Asian economies were successful in diversifying their exports rapidly, and some continue to discover new exports that are sophisticated

Figure 1.5   Export Sophistication and Competitiveness (EXPY) Increase with Level of Secondary Education (Percent of the Labor Force that has Completed Secondary Education)

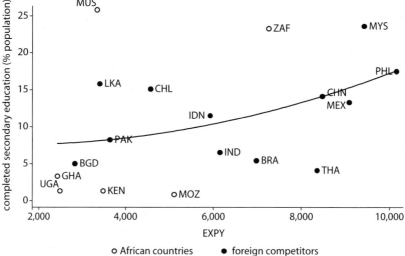

Source: Education corresponds to year 1999 from Barro and Lee (2000) estimates. EXPY was calculated using UN Comtrade SITC Rev. 2–4 digits for 2000–2004.

Notes: BRA-Brazil; BGD-Bangladesh; CHL-Chile; CHN-China; GHA-Ghana; IND-India; IDN-Indonesia; KEN-Kenya; LKA-Sri Lanka; MEX-Mexico; MOZ-Mozambique; MUS-Mauritius; MYS-Malaysia; PAK-Pakistan; PHL-Philippines; THA-Thailand; UGA-Uganda; ZAF-South Africa.

and have high domestic value added. Part of their success lies in the fact that many firms in East Asia belong to global production networks. This involves trading of parts and components between countries during the production process. Such trade has been expanding rapidly since the 1970s. Between 1970 and 1990, trade mediated by value chains accounted for 21 percent of exports and 30 percent of the growth of exports (Hummels, Ishii, and Yi 2001) in East Asia. By being a part of global production networks, firms in East Asia had more opportunities to discover new export goods and adapt speedily through assistance often provided by the lead firms. The role of the lead firm is important, even for garments. Although the garment industry can still provide some opportunities for low-income countries to diversify their exports (despite the dominance by China and India), the rise of global buyers means that exporters need to be part of a network.

A major development in East Asia has been the emergence of giant firms that serve as the nodes of the production networks, helping to knit together many smaller suppliers and performing an intermediary role

Figure 1.6   Progress from Low-value Commodity to High-value Agricultural and Resoures-based Processed Exports, 1985–2004

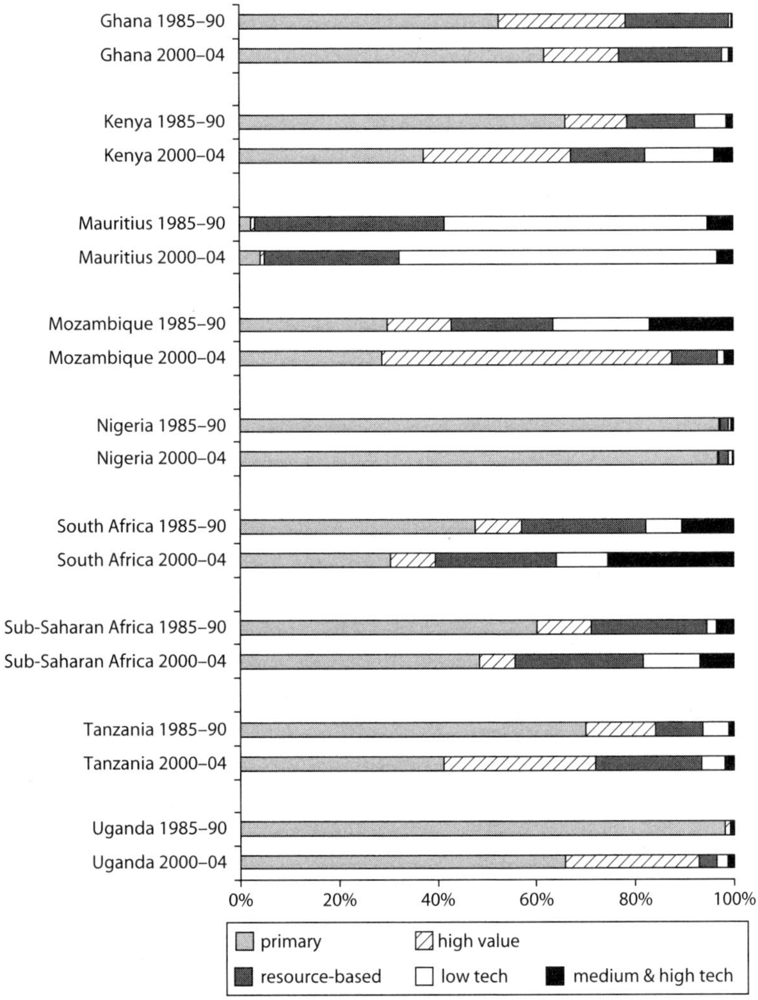

Source: Chandra, Boccardo, and Osorio 2007.

between the buyers and myriad producers scattered across the region. Firms such as Yue Yuen (the world's largest producer of shoes), Hon Hai Precision Industry (the largest contract manufacturer of electronics), and Esquel Group (one of the largest producers of shirts) are examples of such firms. So far, firms in Africa remain outside of such production networks.[54]

Africa's low skill levels constrain its capacity to discover new export options and to diversify into manufactures that are skill intensive, or to

Table 1.8   Export Diversification Trend Indicators in Africa

	Herfindahl Index		Share of top five commodities (%)		Export growth (%)		EXPY	
	1985– 90	2000– 04	1985– 90	2000– 04	1985– 90	2000– 04	1985– 90	2000– 04
Ghana	0.21	0.17	81	70	14	4	2,597	2,560
Kenya	0.17	0.09	67	54	5	6	2,243	3,375
Mauritius	0.14	0.10	67	63	14	3	4,088	3,563
Mozambique	0.08	0.25	47	72	10	26	3,412	3,839
Nigeria	0.87	0.81	97	96	1	14	2,974	3,774
Rest of SSA	0.38	0.35	85	80	5	15	1,575	2,250
South Africa	0.05	0.04	44	37	6	10	5,000	6,551
Tanzania	0.13	0.07	62	49	3	8	1,513	2,365
Uganda	0.69	0.38	92	79	7	3	1,025	2,039

Source: Chandra, Boccardo, and Osorio 2007.
Note: Share of top five commodities denotes the share of the five largest products in total exports. Export growth denotes annual export growth (nominal). EXPY is the Rodrik-Hausmann score of export competitiveness and Sophistication, with a higher number indicating higher sophistication. The data are based on UN Comtrade, SITC Rev 2. – 4 digit level.

export resource-based products in processed form (Wood 1994; Wood and Berge 1997; Wood and Mayer 2001). Natural resource-intensive economies such as Malaysia have embraced agricultural biotechnology so as to increase yields and find new uses for agricultural raw materials, such as palm oil.[55]

Agricultural biotechnology, in addition to helping raise the productivity of staple crops, has the potential to stimulate biotechnology development in neighboring areas related to medicine, for example, which could improve health care in the region (Paarlberg 2008). At this stage, there is scarcely any need to further underline the attraction of a strong agricultural technology sector. China, for instance, which does 20 percent of the global R&D in this field, spends US$400 million a year on such research, a twofold increase over the level in 2003 (*Financial Times* 2007a), and expects to double this investment level again by 2010.

Biotechnology is heavily science based, and usually relies upon universities to provide the key advances in knowledge, the highly skilled researchers to develop the products, and frequently, the academic entrepreneurs to launch commercial enterprises that take research from the laboratory bench into the field, and from there to the market.[56] This is where the role of tertiary institutions becomes crucial. By training technical and professional workers, tertiary institutions can stimulate domestic research and build the "ideas factories" that could enable African countries to extend their recent successes with cut flowers, vegetables, and tree crops, and move beyond those into biofuels, new materials, and medicinal compounds such as *artemisia afra* and the anti-malarial precursor *artemisinin* (Gans and Stern 2003).[57]

Notes

1. Prominent exceptions include various private U.S. foundations (Carnegie, Ford, MacArthur, Rockefeller), the Department for Research Cooperation of the Swedish Agency for Research Cooperation with Developing Countries, the Norwegian Agency for Development (NORAD), the Finnish International Development Agency (FINNIDA), and UNESCO.

2. For the purposes of this report, Sub-Saharan Africa and Africa are used interchangeably.

3. See the OECD Credit Reporting System Aid Activity database at http://www.oecd.org.

4. By 2005, gross primary enrollment for Africa had attained 97 percent (UNESCO 2007).

5. With subspecialties proliferating within industries, the demand for workers with expertise in these specialties is also growing (see Arora, Fosfuri, and Gambardella 2001).

6. In his address to the Economic History Association in 1980, Richard Easterlin (1981) speculated that the spread of economic growth appeared to be linked to the provision of mass education. A United Nations Industrial Development Organization (UNIDO) Industrial Report finds that almost 60 percent of the differences in income levels between SSA countries and industrialized countries can be attributed to the difference in the stock of knowledge. Between 1992 and 2002, 20 percent of the growth in East Asia came from the changes in knowledge stock, while the contribution was negative for SSA (UNIDO 2005). Barro and Sala-i-Martin (1995) show that increasing average male education attainment by 0.68 years yields an increase in GDP growth by 1.1 percentage points, and an increase in tertiary education of 0.09 years raises growth by 0.5 percentage points. Furthermore, lagging countries that raised their stock of education were able to grow much faster. Lin (2004) finds that a 1 percent increase in higher education stock in Taiwan (China) led to a 3.5 percent rise in industrial output, and a 1 percent increase in the number of graduates from engineering or natural sciences led to a 0.15 percent increase in agricultural output. Krueger and Lindahl's (2001) survey establishes the high returns to education based on individual-level data. But this study did not clarify differences between social returns and private returns. Bloom, Hartley, and Rosovsky (2006) show that the

highly educated are more entrepreneurial, and more educated entrepreneurs create more jobs compared to less educated entrepreneurs, and higher education enrollments are correlated with better governance. Heckman (2002) estimates that the return to education in China is between 30 percent and 40 percent. The substantial contribution of skills to Korea's industrial transformation is supported by the findings of Guarini, Molini, and Rabellotti (2006).

7. Historically, the returns to education have been higher compared to returns from physical investments (Psacharopoulos 2006). Social rates of return to tertiary education range from 9.7 percent to 17 percent. While they may be lower than those of primary education, these rates are much higher than returns to physical capital (Azcona and others 2008). The OECD average in 2001 was 8.5 percent, ranging from 4 percent to 14 percent among the 21 OECD countries (Boarini and Strauss 2007). Among selected Latin American countries, the rate of return ranged from 11 percent to 22 percent, most of which is higher than that of secondary education (de Ferranti and others 2003).

8. The reason why the social return to tertiary education is lower than the private return is because public tertiary education is highly subsidized. However, once the definition of "social" benefits is broadened to include safety, democratization, and less corruption (which are hard to quantify), the social rate of return can be higher (Psacharopoulos 2006).

9. See Silles (2007) for the detailed analysis of this for men in the United Kingdom.

10. A growing demand for skilled workers has been observed in the United States also. Lemieux (2007) relates this to the rising returns to postsecondary education in the United States.

11 In addition, the use of private tutoring is becoming a widespread phenomenon globally, suggesting that private returns to education are increasing, especially at the higher levels (Dang and Rogers 2008).

12. See, for instance, Carnoy (2006) on Brazil, China, India, and Russia.

13. This represented a significant downturn of the trends in the 1960s, when per-capita growth rates averaged 2.5 percent, falling to 1.5 percent during 1970–74 (Artadi and Sala-i-Martin 2003). See also Johnson, Ostry, and Subramanian (2007). Some recent research links SSA's current performance with the experience under colonial rule and the institutional changes it either introduced or did not permit (Nunn 2007). A succinct account of SSA's transition from colonial rule to independence, and how this shaped politics and institutions, can be found in Cooper (2002).

14. Even so, economies in Sub-Saharan Africa remain relatively small. Calderisi (2006) writes that "Excluding South Africa, [Sub-Saharan Africa] produces

only as much as Belgium. By 2000, the typical African economy had an income no larger than the suburb of a major American city like Bethesda, Maryland (US$2 billion). . . only a tenth of exports are manufactures . . . tourism is small and shallow—few people return to the continent for a second or third visit—and the list of most popular destinations has remained the same for 40 years."

15. The diversity in rates of growth is discussed by Ndulu and others (2007). How the petroleum exporters can avoid a slowing of growth and a waste of resources associated with the so-called resource curse is usefully explored by the contributors to Humphreys, Sachs, and Stiglitz (2007); by Collier (2007); and by Levy (2007).

16. Informal flows could add more than US$90 billion to the global aggregate (Gupta, Pattillo, and Wagh 2007).

17. In 2005, global remittances amounted to US$188 billion, twice as much as official development assistance. The remittance flow has been growing by 15 percent on average since 2000. Among the top 25 recipient countries, the only country from SSA was Nigeria. The largest recipients are China, India, and Mexico (Gupta, Pattillo, and Wagh 2007). However, since 2000, remittances to SSA countries have grown by 55 percent, and in 2005 the flow to these countries was estimated at US$6.5 billion, accounting for 4 percent of total remittances to developing countries. Remittances can be used for supplementing consumption by the family members in the home country or for investment. The literature on remittances, especially at the aggregate level, consistently finds that the motivation for remittances is mainly to support consumption by family members in the home country. Using a panel data set, Chami, Fullenkamp, and Jahjah (2005) find that remittance flows are countercyclical in nature, supporting consumption-based motives rather than investment-based ones. In addition, some studies find a potential moral hazard problem—that is, recipient family members increasingly rely on remittances for their consumption needs (Azam and Gubert 2006). Studies based on household surveys do find some instances where remittances are used for investment such as housing and education (Adams 2006; Salisu 2005). While remittances may not have a direct growth effect on investment, Aggarwal, Demirguc-Kunt, and Peria (2006) show that remittance flows contribute to the development of the financial sector. For a recent review of migration and remittances, see Page and Plaza (2006).

18. A more detailed look at the top five export commodities in engineering, food, and garments reveals that the baskets of commodities in these subsectors fluctuate fairly widely, except in Mauritius and South Africa. This suggests that while these countries do have the basic capability to produce these commodities, they are a limited and fluctuating source of revenues. Exports from these countries rise only when global supplies are temporarily squeezed, and then

diminish once again. This suggests that export competitiveness of these countries in manufactures is fairly low.

19. Rising food prices during 2000–07 did not have an adverse effect on terms of trade because of the high price of other commodities. However, countries are facing inflationary pressure that adversely affects the poor, especially in urban areas, and the acceleration of food grain prices in 2008 is a worrying development (World Bank 2008f). Between 2000 and 2006, worldwide demand for cereals increased by 8 percent, but prices rose by 50 percent because supply response was sluggish until 2007–08, and biofuel production ate into the supply of corn (*Financial Times* 2008). The price of rice has more than doubled since 2004 (*Oxford Analytica* 2008c) and prices of wheat and soybeans have doubled in the last two years (*Oxford Analytica* 2008d). This has prompted, on the one hand, the importing countries to reduce or eliminate import tariffs on food items. On the other hand, many exporting countries such as Argentina, India, and Vietnam, are imposing export taxes or disallowing exports so as to curb the rise of domestic food prices, which leads to further upward pressure on international prices (*Economist* 2008a,b,c,d). Some countries, such as China, have introduced price controls to contain the price of food and inputs such as fertilizer (*Oxford Analytica* 2008a). Rising food prices are forcing aid organization such as the World Food Programme and the U.S. Agency for International Development to ask for additional funding of US$500 million and US$350 million, respectively (*Economist* 2008b). High food prices are expected to persist at least until 2015 (World Bank 2008f).

20. Governance and corruption indicators for SSA do not convey a reassuring picture of progress over the past decade. A modest overall improvement in accountability and political stability are offset by deteriorating governance indicators in many countries, including five of the seven in our sample. Only Mauritius and South Africa have registered gains since 1996 (Economist Intelligence Unit 2006d). Corruption has worsened throughout the region. The average score for SSA countries on this index-fell from 3.3 in 2001 to 2.8 in 2006. With the exception again of Mauritius and South Africa, the other five countries had low scores and rankings in 2006. However, except for Ghana, all raised their scores between 2001 and 2006 (Economist Intelligence Unit 2006c).

21. The drag on growth exerted by high transaction costs is discussed by Ndulu and others (2007).

22. With reference to Latin America, Edwards (2007, p. 22) is pessimistic that growth prospects will improve because "countries in the region show no political willingness to embark on reforms required to strengthen their institutions." This is pertinent for many African countries as well.

23. As Freeman and Lindauer (1999) point out, past growth was driven in large part by physical capital, not human capital. For example, growth accounting

estimates show that 10 percent of the growth in Korea was due to human capital (Lee 2006). However, Devarajan, Easterly, and Pack (2003) find that in Africa, the link between investment and growth is not as strong as in East Asia because of other factors that can render investments unproductive.

24. The worth of supply chains is now widely recognized because they frequently are able to deliver better value to customers. Fung, Fung, and Wind (2008) rightly observe that "network participation [yields] tangible and intangible benefits such as learning, trust, access to global clients and long-term business development" (p. 49). Networks make it easier to solve problems and to pool capacity so as to more readily and quickly meet demand. African producers can benefit from networks because agricultural value-added per worker in Sub-Saharan Africa at US$343 in 2004 was the lowest in the world. The world average is close to US$900, and that of Latin America is more than US$3,000 (J.E.Austin Associates 2007). See J.E.Austin Associates (2007) for a detailed look at the agriculture in Sub-Saharan Africa, and for an assessment of tools and approaches that can be used to guide agricultural development.

25. Gibbon and Ponte (2005) are of the view that the dismantling of African parastatals reduced the bargaining power of local producers and the ability to implement quality controls.

26. As Arora, Fosfuri, and Gambardella (2001) point out, many companies, such as GE are sitting on a storehouse of unutilized patents that could be licensed to others. IBM has taken the lead in making many of its patents available at no cost to other users.

27. Transgenic crops offer many advantages, among them being resistance to disease, improved nutritional content, longer shelf life, reduced bruising during transport, etc. (Graff, Roland-Holst, and Zilberman 2006). But given the many technical development and certification barriers, most SSA countries are 10 to 15 years from deriving benefits from genetically modified crops (Eicher, Maredia, and Sithole-Niang 2006).

28. On the performance and growth of the furniture industry in China, see Robb and Xie (2003).

29. See Caesar, Jens, and Seitz (2007) on the opportunities in biofuels.

30. For example, expert software programs that simplify diagnostics of equipment and of human ailments could help contain the need for skilled workers, while at the same time raising the quality of maintenance and health care.

31. This could lead to a shift from crop to pastoral farming and a preference for sheep and goat herding over the rearing of chickens and cattle (Seo and Mendelson 2007).

32. Watson, Zinyowera, and Moss 2007; Stern 2007.

33. The problems posed by AIDS, malaria, and other diseases in Africa have been exhaustively researched and the literature does not need to be summarized

here. Suffice it to say that infectious diseases are hobbling SSA's economic performance, sustaining high levels of fertility as families try to ensure that they have a few surviving children, and storing up future social problems in the form of orphans, workers whose development in early childhood was affected by disease, and large youth cohorts with limited job prospects (Kalemli-Ozcan 2006; Conley, McCord, and Sachs 2007; Haacker 2007). In 2005, 6.1 percent of the population of SSA in the 15 to 55 age groups was HIV positive. Worldwide, malaria is the cause of 300 million to 500 million infections each year, and 90 percent of those cases are in SSA. It annually kills 1 million people, mainly children, the majority of whom are in Africa (5 percent of all children in SSA are killed by malaria, and the average age-specific mortality is 4 years). The toll inflicted by the disease annually worldwide is US$12 billion (Johns Hopkins Malaria Research Institute 2007). By one estimate, reducing the damage inflicted by malaria will require on outlay of US$3.2 billion annually, less than US$800 million of which has been committed to date (*Financial Times* 2007b). Johnson, Ostry, and Subramanian (2007) also comment on the drag exerted by health-related problems.

34. Jimenez and Murthi (2006) claim that with appropriate investment in human capital, the bulge could become the basis of an economic boom. In the case of Sub-Saharan Africa, by 2025, an estimated 258 million workers will be reaching prime working age (15–24 years), potentially providing the continent with a "demographic bonus" (Azcona and others 2008). The 2007 *World Development Report* offers detailed suggestions as to how the youth bulge could be productively harnessed (World Bank 2007c). Urdal's (2006) cross-country study shows, however, that such bulges greatly increase the risk of political violence (see also Gavin 2007).

35. In recent years, being landlocked seems to matter somewhat less as long as the goods exported can be transported by air and are of higher value. This is even true for commodity exports. For instance, Uganda was successful in using air transport to export fresh fruits and organic products that meet EU standards (Chandra, Boccardo, and Osorio 2007). How this will evolve if energy costs continue to rise and climate change begins to impact upon the viability of certain agricultural activities, is difficult to say. But much will depend on economic flexibility, the speed of adaptation, and the fundamental resilience of the various countries, and this ultimately will be a matter of skills and institutions. The recovery of Japan and Germany after WWII was largely a function of the above.

36. Broadman (2007) observes that 40 percent of the population of SSA is in landlocked countries versus 23 percent of the population of Eastern Europe and the former Soviet Union.

37. Studies find that the returns from agricultural research are high, ranging from 16 percent to 135 percent in Sub-Saharan Africa. However, weak linkages

between research institutes and farmers resulted in less than 10 percent of the new crop varieties developed by the research institutes being adopted by farmers (Azcona and others 2008).

38. For instance, Mozambique in 1990 had less than 3,000 university graduates, and less than 15 percent of its civil servants held university degrees. With the expansion of the university sector, there are now more than 600 graduates coming out of the system each year, leading to general skill upgrading in both private and public sectors (World Bank Institute 2007).

39. This also underlies the "failed state" problem discussed by Collier (2007) and by many others.

40. See Beck and Levine (2002), who underscore the contribution of financial deepening backed by a strengthening of legal institutions.

41. Fourteen years ago, the *World Development Report 1994* (World Bank 1994) observed that by neglecting to undertake US$12 billion of preventive maintenance of fixed assets, SSA countries were saddled with a US$45 billion outlay for reconstruction. Later research by Charles Hulten (1996) indicated that the effectiveness of infrastructure suitably measured, exerted a strong influence on growth. When Hulten contrasted the performance of East Asian economies with those in SSA, one-quarter of the difference in growth rates— about 0.75 percent per annum—was explained by how efficiently the infrastructure was utilized. The poor state of roads in SSA gravely diminishes trade and increases transport costs, including wear on vehicles. If the quality of South Africa's roads is set at 100, then Nigeria's are rated at 34, Ghana's at 30, and Kenya's, Uganda's, and Tanzania's at less than 20. Tanzania rates the lowest at 6.4 (Economist Intelligence Unit 2007b). Estimates by the World Bank suggest that SSA needs about US$20 billion in new infrastructure investment to narrow the deficit (*Financial Times* 2006). Investing in infrastructure and maintaining its operational quality could raise the growth by 2.3 percentage points (Calderon 2008). Equally important is the need to improve the management and maintenance of the current stock of infrastructure and new additions. This requires both managerial and technical skills.

42. Developing countries must now cope with technologies (typically embedded in imported machinery) being devised that reflect the evolving and higher order skill mix in developed countries. Hence, when developing countries import these capital goods, they typically lack the necessary skills to use them efficiently (Acemoglu 2002; Acemoglu and Zilibotti 2001). While research has tended to focus on the "hard" technologies, the situation is no different for "soft" technologies, i.e. regulation, pricing, finance, legal, risk and asset management, etc.

43. According to the Investment Climate Assessment surveys by the World Bank, one-quarter of all managers in Africa had earned a postgraduate degree, 7 percent had a technical degree, and 30 percent had some university education. The share of managers with a secondary degree was 30 percent—equally

divided between vocational and nonvocational education. Less than 2 percent had no education. By comparison, more than 80 percent of managers in Chile and China had some university education. Managers of most exporting firms are likely to have a postgraduate education. Large- and medium-size firms have more managers with university or postgraduate degrees, while small firms and nonexporters rely more on managers with a secondary school degree. Not surprisingly, in South Africa and Mauritius, more than 34 percent of the managers have a postgraduate degree. In contrast, in Uganda, a country with the highest share of managers in its workforce in SSA, few have a postgraduate degree. In general, most SSA managers had received a degree from a foreign university; only 10 percent had a local university degree. India paid particular attention to management education from the 1950s. The intake capacity for postgraduates in management was 83,000 in 2005 (Chandra, Boccardo, and Osorio 2007). Although India has been emphasizing management education, it is still facing a shortage of qualified personnel to teach. The current estimate of such shortage is about 6,000, with a present output of only 150 doctorates in management per year.

44. Between 1995 and 2000, growth of labor productivity averaged 2.7 percent per annum, almost half derived from efficiency gains. This rose to 3.4 percent per annum during 2000–05; 56 percent was from improvements in efficiency (Council of Economic Advisors 2007). Other countries also had access to new technologies and comparable skill ratios, but the United States has retained a lead in productivity and growth because of the quality of the skills employed in allocating and utilizing resources and market competitiveness (Gordon 2003, 2004a,b; on the euro see McMorrow and Roger 2007).

45. The principal European economies have higher capital intensity and fewer semiskilled or unskilled workers (Crafts 2007).

46. Since 1991, the annual contribution of human capital to growth in SSA has risen to 0.4 percent (Ndulu and others 2007).

47. Botswana, for instance, lost 17 percent of its health care workers between 1999 and 2005 because of mortality related to HIV/AIDS (Connell and others 2007).

48. The demand for health care workers is rising globally, and as a consequence, many developing countries are faced with increasing emigration of health care workers, including those from Sub-Saharan Africa. Traditionally, the sending countries have been Nigeria and South Africa, but in recent years, emigration is increasing from Ghana, Kenya, and Uganda. As a region, Sub-Saharan Africa has the highest emigration rates, followed by South Asia (Mullan 2005). Before World War II, the flow was actually from developed to developing countries, but the direction is now reversed. In the United States, the number

of foreign-trained doctors increased from 70,646 in 1973 to 210,000 in 2003. In the United Kingdom, the number of foreign-trained doctors increased from 20,923 in 1970 to 69,813 in 2003. In these two countries, foreign-trained workers account for more than 30 percent of all health care workers (Connell and others 2007).

49. In fact, emigration is an incentive for individuals to seek tertiary-level education, and an increase in the skilled unemployed, which increases job search activity domestically, can improve the match between skills and jobs (Stark and Fan 2007).

50. Imbs and Wacziarg (2003) find that the relationship between economic diversification and economic development is U-shaped, with the inflection point at about US$10,000 (in 2000 U.S. dollars); that is, lower income countries tend to diversify their export basket before they begin to specialize. Once they reach middle-income level, countries start to specialize, mainly on higher value-added goods. However, the faster growing economies are the ones that move quickly to the next stage of diversification (Hesse 2006; Chandra, Boccardo, and Osorio 2007).

51. A survey by Wagner finds that overall, firms that are more productive tend to start exporting. The results also suggest that firms consciously adopt strategies to improve their capabilities so that they can export in the future (Wagner 2007).

52. The rationale behind the calculation of the weighted average of per-capita income of an exporting country is to capture the unobservable quality and technological sophistication of these goods. The higher the value, the higher the quality and the sophistication needed to produce and export these goods.

53. Only a few African countries are prominent producers of high-value agricultural products exported mainly to the EU. These include Ethiopia (cut flowers and coffee), Kenya (fresh vegetables and cut flowers), Madagascar and the Comoros (vanilla and cloves), Mozambique and Malawi (nuts), South Africa (citrus, apples, table grapes), and Uganda and Tanzania (fish fillets). See Kjollerstrom and Dallto (2007) for a detailed discussion of resource-based exports.

54. For instance, Brenton and Hoppe (2007) find that firms in Africa do not export as much as their model predicts.

55. See also Weir and Knight (2007) on how the education levels of the farming community shift the production frontier and induce innovation.

56. A promising start with "green chemistry" based on crops such as enset and cassava has been made at the University of Addis Ababa, and it has considerable promise for hydrocarbon resource-poor countries because it seeks to replace hazardous products and processes with less hazardous ones (*Science* 2007).

57. *Artemisia afra* has been an ingredient of African herbal medicines for generations and is used to treat minor disorders. Experimentation with the cultivation of *artemisia annua* (or sweet wormwood)—a plant that is native to the mountainous regions of southwestern China—began almost a decade ago. By 2006, 1,000 hectares were planted with *artemisia annua* in Kenya, Tanzania, and Uganda. A company called Advanced Bio Extracts, with operating entities in all three countries, now works with the farmers to ensure continuous supplies and expand cultivation. Its manufacturing facility, which extracts and purifies the compound, is located at Athi River in Kenya. The company supplies the Swiss pharmaceutical firm Novartis (which provides both technical and financial support), the producer of the ACT antimalarial drug Coartem (*The Nation* (Kenya) 2004).

CHAPTER 2

The Education Imperative

In many SSA countries, literacy and primary enrollments have risen to the point where they have ceased to be binding constraints on economic performance. Future development is predicated more than in the past on the level and quality of secondary education, and the upgrading and supply of tertiary-level skills. With each passing year, the knowledge content of almost every industrial field is becoming richer, and the technological thresholds of most industrial activities are rising. The capabilities of the workforce must rise commensurately. Not just industrializing but also developed countries are recognizing that if knowledge is the arbiter of economic advancement, the preparedness of secondary school graduates and the training of tertiary students must rank among the highest priorities for economic policy making.[1]

Successful countries such as Korea (and more recently, China) have been able to rapidly expand the supply of skilled workers and dramatically alter the education profile of their populations. In contrast, many countries in SSA have failed to do so (see figure 2.1, which presents the contrasting profiles for Korea and Ghana).

Secondary school enrollments in SSA, while rising, are still quite low. Tertiary-level enrollments are well below levels necessary to accelerate industrial deepening and export diversification (see figure 2.2). Furthermore,

Figure 2.1   Changes in Education Profile in Korea and Ghana, 1960–2000

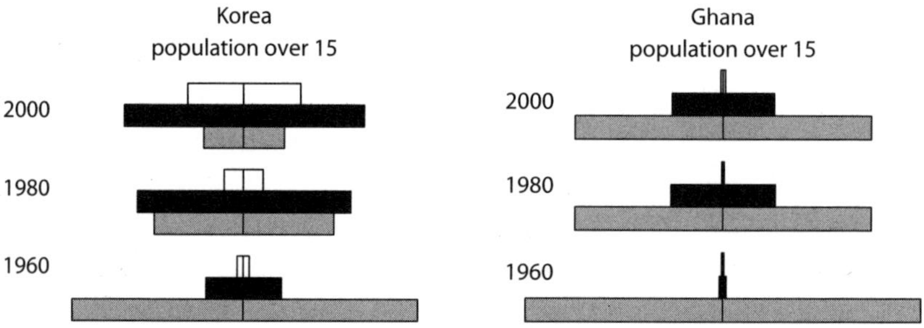

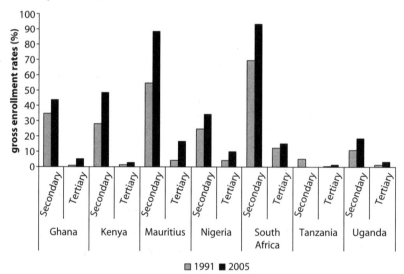

Source: Barro and Lee 2000.
Note: The top block represents the percentage of the population with tertiary education, the middle block represents the percentage of the population with only secondary education, and the bottom block represents the percentage of the population with only primary education.

Figure 2.2   Secondary and Tertiary Gross Enrollment Rates for Case Study Countries, 1991 and 2005

Sources: World Development Indicators (2006) and EdStat.
Note: Data for tertiary enrollment in Kenya from 1990 and 2004; data for tertiary enrollment in Nigeria from 1992 and 2004; data for secondary enrollment in South Africa from 2004; data for tertiary enrollment in Uganda from 2004.

the results from the latest international test scores on mathematics and science at the secondary level reveal that scores in Botswana, Ghana, and South Africa are much lower than the international average (see table 2.1). This suggests that efforts to raise educational quality at the secondary level

Table 2.1   Average Math and Science Scores of Eighth-Grade Students in Selected Countries, 2003

Country	Math score	Science score
Korea	589	558
Malaysia	508	510
International average	**466**	**473**
Jordan	424	475
Indonesia	411	420
Egypt	406	421
Chile	387	413
Botswana	366	365
Ghana	276	255
South Africa	264	244

Source: National Center for Education Statistics (2004).
Note: Four international benchmarks are defined: the advanced benchmark is 625, the high benchmark is 550, the intermediate benchmark is 475, and the low benchmark is 400.

will produce benefits at the tertiary level in terms of student preparedness for study and employment.

We plot the data for a sample of countries in SSA and a few comparators in figures 2.3 and 2.4. The line in figures 2.3 and 2.4 indicate the predicted level of enrollment given the per-capita income. Enrollment in secondary education is greater than that predicted only in Ghana, Kenya, and South Africa. For tertiary education, only the gross enrollments in Nigeria and Uganda are higher than predicted by the model. Gross enrollments in secondary education are below predicted values in fast-growing countries such as Malaysia, Mauritius, and Thailand. Gross enrollments in tertiary education are also much below the predicted values for Mauritius and South Africa, and to a lesser extent for Malaysia, while in other countries they are close to the predicted value given the income level. The explanation arguably lies in the preference for quality over quantity in some of the economically dynamic countries that fall below the trend line. However, looking ahead, the desirable options for development call for increases in the level and quality of tertiary education. A point on the historical trend line (which represents the average level of achievement in the past) is no longer adequate for countries aiming for rapid growth; instead it is desirable to aim for a higher level of enrollment.

Fortunately, an opportunity to pursue the education imperative has emerged. The recent acceleration of growth, and the promise of additional external assistance, will potentially enlarge the resource envelope for SSA countries. The region is politically more stable than at any time in the recent past and less troubled by civil strife. Regarding climate change,

Figure 2.3   Secondary Gross Enrollment in 2004

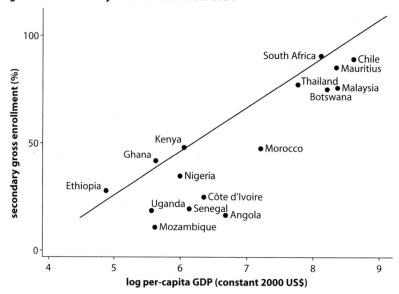

Source: Authors' calculations.
Note: The predicted value is based on a regression of 105 low- and middle-income countries, weighted by the population. Data for South Africa and Malaysia are from 2003; for Angola from 2001; and for Côte d'Ivoire from 2001. All data are from the World Development Indicators.

Africa has a 15- to 20- year window to begin introducing technologies and building the hard and soft infrastructures needed to accommodate the major structural changes that will be needed. By investing in secondary and tertiary education and maintaining a high level of investment in this sector, African countries can:

- ensure that the volume and quality of skills needed—many highly specialized—will be forthcoming, possibly with a gestation lag of a decade (with substantial reliance initially on overseas training);[2] capitalize on the youth bulge; and if education does improve employment prospects, neutralize the likelihood that the underemployed will stoke violence.
- deepen the institutional base for research in universities and specialized institutes.
- initiate the process of technology development on a much larger scale, as well as technology transfer between research centers and the business and agricultural sectors.

Figure 2.4   Tertiary Gross Enrollment in 2004

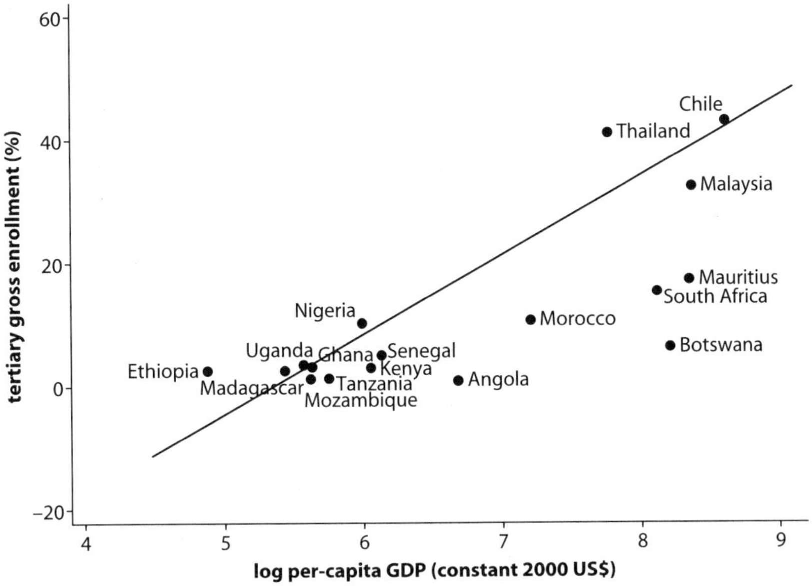

Source: Authors' calculations.
Note: The predicted value is based on a regression of 86 low- and middle-income countries, weighted by the population. Data for Angola, Malaysia, and South Africa, are from 2003. All data are from the World Development Indicators.

These results cannot be obtained on the cheap because the demand for tertiary education is very strong;[3] quality must rise, replacing retiring faculty and attracting new talent to augment teaching staffs; and a large backlog of investment in infrastructure must be addressed. For these reasons, there is a need to funnel additional resources into tertiary education for a period of at least a decade to offset past shortfalls, and to compensate for the large current stock of workers with weak skills who cannot cost-effectively be retrained. This public spending can then return to the existing levels, which is comparable to spending by other countries.[4] Hence, adequate financing from public and private sources will be key.[5] Resources alone will not do the trick without parallel reforms that lead to a more efficient allocation of these resources; improve the curriculum, pedagogical practices, and soft skills of tertiary institutions; and strengthen their autonomy as well as governance structures (Hanushek and Woessmann 2007; World Bank 2007).[6] Moreover, all of this will have to be undertaken within the larger dynamics of the demand for and supply of tertiary graduates.

The Demand for Higher-level Skills in Sub-Saharan Africa

Social demand. Most Africans view educational achievement as the principal pathway to success in life. Consequently, the social demand for access, particularly at the upper levels of education, is unrelenting. This creates strong political pressures for expansion and impedes the reforms needed to maintain quality and competitiveness.[7] The public's demand for tertiary education is shaped in part by overall trends in population growth, and in part by trends in access at the lower educational levels. The youth population in Sub-Saharan Africa, already more than four times its 1950 level, is projected to continue growing rapidly into the foreseeable future (World Bank 2007a). Over the past 15 years, population growth rates have begun to slow somewhat in Anglophone Africa, but have remained high in Francophone Africa (figure 2.5). As a result, growth projections for the tertiary-level age cohort (20 to 24 years) suggest that demographic pressures on tertiary education will ease sooner within the Anglophone countries than within the Francophone

Figure 2.5   Population Growth Rates in Anglophone and Francophone Africa, 1990–2005

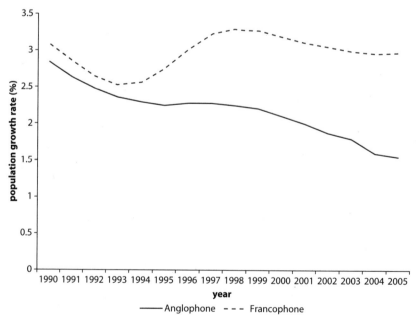

Sources: World Bank, UNESCO Institute of Statistics 2008.

countries. Specifically, the expected growth in the tertiary-age population, as projected in five-year intervals from 2010 through 2050, will fall below 10 percent for Anglophone countries in 2015, but Francophone countries will have to wait until 2040 before their tertiary-age growth rate declines to this level (figure 2.6).

In the meantime, broadening access to lower levels of education is expected to maintain the rising trends of recent years (figure 2.7), thus intensifying the pressure for access to tertiary education. Fueling this pressure will be the emerging trend for governments to offer universal secondary education, already manifest in Ghana, Kenya, Tanzania, and Uganda. Only 25 percent or less of qualified secondary school leavers currently obtain university access in Ghana, Kenya, Nigeria, Tanzania, and elsewhere, and this competition will certainly intensify. As a result, most governments will not be able financially to maintain current rates of expansion in tertiary enrollments and upgrade quality without significant changes to the present structure and financing of their tertiary systems (Mingat, Ledoux, and Rakotomalala 2008).

Labor market demand. In an analysis of graduate employment trends in Africa, Mingat and Majgaard (2008) note that secondary and tertiary

Figure 2.6   Projected Growth Rate of 20- to 24-year-old Population for Anglophone and Francophone Africa, 2010–50

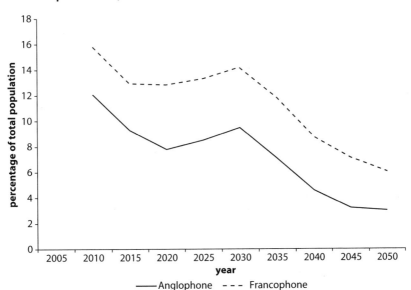

Sources: World Bank, UNESCO Institute of Statistics 2008.

Figure 2.7   GER Index by Level of Education, 1990–2005

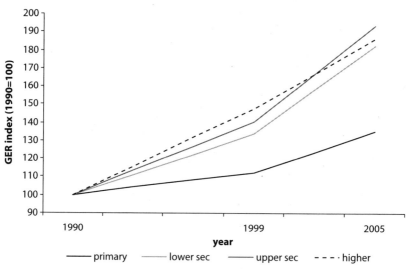

Source: Mingat and Majgaard 2008.

graduates are employed primarily by the public sector, which accounts for just 4.1 percent of total regional employment. The modern private sector (5.4 percent of total regional employment) currently makes little use of highly skilled workers.[8] This suggests a potential for productivity increases through an upgrading of skill profiles among workers. But because the modern private sector is growing only at the same rate as the labor force, its absorptive capacity will be limited, and rising graduate unemployment is a risk—unless, of course, the infusion of higher-skilled and entrepreneurial workers induces new starts of more technology-intensive firms that in turn employ more graduates.

Feedback from employers supports the need for more relevant tertiary teaching and research. Employer surveys report that tertiary graduates are weak in problem-solving, business understanding, computer use, communication, and teamwork skills. A "total lack of practical skills among technology graduates" was reported by employers in Nigeria (World Bank 2006). Similar complaints were voiced by Ghanaian firms (Boateng and Ofori-Sarpong 2002).

Although the call for better prepared graduates is unequivocal, the extent to which this translates into higher graduate employment is unclear. On the one hand, we have evidence of relatively low graduate unemployment in Africa. The Institute of Development Studies of the

University of Sussex in 2001 conducted tracer studies of 2,500 university graduates from 1980, 1987, 1994, and 1999 in Malawi, Tanzania, Uganda, and Zimbabwe. It found that unemployment rates among graduates were quite low (1 percent to 3 percent) and that most graduates were generally employed in their field of university studies (Al-Samarrai and Bennell 2003). Similarly, 10 tracer studies with 6,100 total responses undertaken in Ghana, Kenya, Malawi, Nigeria, Tanzania, and Uganda during 1996–98[9] reported an overall unemployment rate of 5 percent, with slightly higher rates for science and humanities graduates than for those from business, education, and engineering (Mugabushaka, Schomburg, and Teichler 2007).

On the other hand, evidence of high graduate unemployment is equally available. Mismatches between the education provided and capabilities required in the job market reportedly contribute to high graduate unemployment in some countries, e.g., 35 percent in Mauritania and 17 percent in Nigeria (Oni 2005; Teferra and Altbach 2003). In several African countries, the higher the graduate's level of education, the higher the incidence of graduate unemployment. This is the case in Cameroon, Côte d'Ivoire, Madagascar, Mauritania, Niger, Nigeria, Senegal, and Uganda (Amelewonou and Brossard 2005).

One of the few available comparative studies of SSA graduate employment finds that cross-country variation is very large. Based on an assessment of 23 countries for which labor market data were available, Mingat and Majgaard (2008) show that nine of the 23 countries have less than 10 percent unemployment among higher education graduates age 25–34, five countries have between 10 and 20 percent unemployment in this group, and another nine countries have more than 20 percent unemployment. Strikingly, eight of the nine countries characterized by high graduate unemployment are Francophone, presumably as a consequence of their open admission policies.

The graduate unemployment question is clearly a candidate for further study in SSA countries. Major research questions include: To what extent is graduate unemployment determined by the size and vibrancy of a country's economy? Are graduates unemployed because there are few jobs that require their educational level, or because their education and training do not match labor market needs? Is the quality of their skills an issue? Are graduates accepting jobs outside of their professions or in the informal sector? To what extent do graduates know how to find job opportunities? In addition, stakeholders might consider the examples of tertiary education systems in Chile, Colombia, Latvia, Mexico, Morocco,

Sri Lanka, and Vietnam, as well as the European Union, which have set up "labor market observatories" to monitor graduate employment trends and seek feedback on graduate performance.[10]

In general, when graduates do succeed in obtaining employment, the first thing that their employers often have to do is provide them with extensive in-house training (i.e., six to 12 months) before they can be productive on the job, although less than half of firms do so in Africa (Chandra, Boccardo, and Osorio 2007). This raises costs, reduces competitiveness, and underlines the necessity of improving the quality of tertiary education through a significant outlay of resources. In addition, some research suggests that employment of too few tertiary graduates (presumably of acceptable quality) reduces the capacities for innovation within a firm and thus reinforces technical stagnation. This points to a role for government policy in encouraging firms to consider hiring workers with tertiary-level education (Lundvall 2007). The prevailing alternative, where government itself tries to absorb unemployed graduates, as has often occurred in Africa, has had no appreciable effect on the innovative capacity of the economy (Lundvall 2007).

To ensure that enough talented secondary school graduates are drawn into the priority areas of tertiary education and then stay in the country once they graduate, or return after study abroad, as has happened in many East Asian countries (see Saxenian 2006; Yusuf and others 2003; Montgomery and Rondinelli 1995), the government will initially have to prime demand for tertiary-level skills through scholarships, subsidized placement of graduates (including employment at public research institutes), and spending on technology development—building up to at least 1 percent of GDP, directly or through incentives to the private sector (Romer 2000; Lundvall 2007). In the absence of such demand, accompanied with the offer of decently paid jobs, few students will enroll in science and engineering courses and even fewer of those who graduate will remain in the country.

The Supply Profile for Tertiary Education in Africa

Sub-Saharan Africa currently enrolls 4 million tertiary students. This number is triple what it was in 1991. It represents one of the highest regional growth rates in the world for tertiary enrollments, averaging 8.7 percent a year. At this rate, current enrollment numbers will double in eight years. The continent's tertiary enrollment gains produced a gross enrollment ratio (GER) of 4.9 percent in 2005, up from 2.6 percent in 1991. But this regional average masks a significant difference in tertiary access between Francophone and Anglophone countries.[11] As shown in figure 2.8, access has been expanding more rapidly within the Anglophone sphere. The tertiary gross enrollment ratio for Anglophone countries averaged 6.7 percent, in comparison to the 2.9 percent that characterized Francophone nations. Despite rapid enrollment growth, Africa's GER remained the lowest in the world, trailing South Asia (10 percent), East Asia (19 percent), and North Africa and the Middle East (23 percent). Although Africa is running hard, the gap is closing slowly, due in part to high rates of population growth.

Enrollments were distributed among the fields of study shown in table 2.2. On average, just 28 percent of students were enrolled in science and technology fields in 2005 (i.e., agriculture, health science, engineering, sciences). This indicates that much of Africa's recent enrollment growth (including that in private provision) has occurred in the less expensive "soft" disciplines supported by the expansion of private institutions, a

Figure 2.8   Trends in SSA Tertiary GER, 2000–05

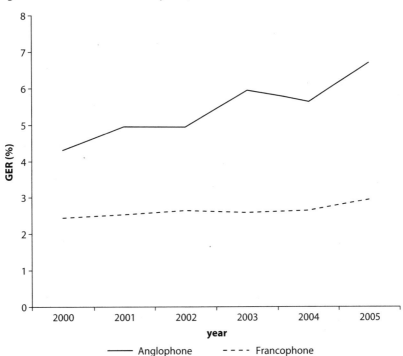

Sources: World Bank, UNESCO Institute of Statistics 2008.

**Table 2.2   Distribution of African University Graduates by
Field of Study, 2005**

Field of study	Distribution of graduates (%)
Agriculture	3
Education	22
Health science	7
Engineering	9
Sciences	9
Social sciences and humanities	47
Other	3

Source: World Bank EdStats.

trend that is unlikely to provide the knowledge and core skills needed if African nations are to boost competitiveness and growth.

Comparing trends in science and technology (S&T) enrollments over nearly two decades for the 23 African countries for which this information is available, declining proportions are observed in 11 of these countries (see table 2.3).[12] Rising shares of S&T enrollments were recorded in another 10 countries, with Nigeria leading this group. For the declining group, more conscious efforts to manage the proportion of S&T enrollments would seem indicated.

Private higher education. A significant portion of Africa's enrollment expansion can be explained by the emergence of a private tertiary education sector on the continent over the past two decades. Since 1990, private colleges, universities, and tertiary-level professional institutes have been established at a far faster rate than public ones.[13] While public universities doubled from roughly 100 to nearly 200 between 1990 and 2007, the number of private tertiary institutions exploded during the same period, from two dozen to an estimated 468 (see Annex A). Non-university tertiary institutions have been the fastest-growing segment within the private tertiary sector, possibly because they offer short-cycle courses that are strongly oriented toward employment (Varghese 2008), or perhaps because they offer a "safe haven" from staff strikes and student demonstrations (Kapur and Crowley 2008).

Slightly over half of private tertiary providers are located in Francophone countries, one-third are in Anglophone countries, and the rest are in countries of other linguistic backgrounds. Senegal leads in the number of private tertiary institutions with 41, followed by the Democratic Republic of the Congo (39), and Nigeria (34). Many of these institutions attract modest enrollments, and the majority have less than

Table 2.3   Share of Tertiary Students Enrolled in Science and Technology Disciplines, by Country

Country	1986–89	2003–04	Change
Angola	64	38	–
Benin	21	30	+
Botswana	9	23	+
Burkina Faso	32	32	0
Burundi	30	26	–
Cameroon	32	33	0
Central African Republic	27	36	+
Chad	12	17	+
Congo, Republic of	13	13	0
Ethiopia	40	31	–
Ghana	42	35	–
Kenya	32	47	+
Lesotho	10	13	+
Madagascar	43	35	–
Malawi	17	59	+
Mali	42	33	–
Mozambique	61	37	–
Niger	31	29	0
Nigeria	39	58	+
Rwanda	26	20	–
Senegal	39	26	–
Togo	24	12	–
Uganda	22	18	–
Average	31	31	

Sources: Brossard and Foko 2006; Saint 1992; Teferra and Altbach 2003.

1,000 students, but their proportion of women students is often higher than in public institutions. The share of private tertiary enrollments in total enrollments is roughly 24 percent in the region as a whole,[14] with private enrollments comprising 19 percent of enrollments in Francophone countries and 32 percent in Anglophone countries (Brossard and Foko 2007). Ownership is generally one of three types: religious nonprofit; secular nonprofit; or secular for-profit. Very few are of transnational origin (Varghese 2008), although one exception is the recently established campus of the private Limkokwing University of Creative Technology (Malaysia) in Botswana.

This trend is echoed at the international level, where private higher education has become the "fastest growing segment of higher education worldwide" (Altbach 2005a). Private providers have long dominated tertiary education in East Asia, where they account for 70 percent or more of enrollments in Japan, Korea, the Philippines, and Taiwan (China). In Latin

America, private provision has expanded rapidly, now enrolling half of tertiary students in Argentina, Brazil, Chile, Colombia, Mexico, Peru, and Venezuela (Altbach 2005b). It is even taking root in Europe, until recently the bastion of public higher education. Private institutions now account for one-third of the total in 13 European countries, with private providers in Portugal and Poland constituting 70 percent of tertiary institutions and serving 28 percent of enrollments (Fried, Glass, and Baumgartl 2007).

Private higher education tends to display common features across geographical regions. Its growth is fueled by massification pressures; its programs emphasize social sciences, economics/business, and law because of their lower start-up costs; it undertakes relatively little research; it frequently employs "moonlighting" academic staff from public universities; it is often religiously affiliated; it is usually located in major urban areas; and it tends to respond to student interests rather than labor market demand (Altbach 2005a; Fried, Glass, and Baumgartl 2007). As a result, private tertiary education is apt to operate beyond the bounds of the coordinated policy framework that steers public tertiary education. This has prompted growing government concern with quality assurance, initially as a way of guaranteeing the standards of private providers, but more recently as a means of ensuring that the nation's overall tertiary system remains competitive on the world scene.

Where government regulation of private tertiary education is enabling rather than controlling, it can play an important role in assuring consumers that they are obtaining educational value for their money, and in expanding access to education more quickly than would otherwise be possible solely on the basis of public funding. Among the enabling mechanisms that governments can employ are direct financial subsidies for the installation of utilities and educational infrastructure, tax holidays during an initial start-up period, customs duty waivers, the provision of land at no charge or at discounted prices, matching grants for information and communications technology (ICT) infrastructure, public scholarships for private students, and public research grants for private researchers (Fielden and LaRocque 2008).

The Mission of Tertiary Education in an Economic Growth Context

Since their founding, African universities and, to a lesser extent, other tertiary institutions, have been guided by the threefold mandate to teach, do research, and serve the community. With only minor variations, these remained the principal missions of tertiary institutions as they entered the twenty-first century (Ajayi, Goma, and Johnson 1996). Tertiary-level teaching has traditionally been provided at residential campuses to secondary school graduates, generally between the ages of 18 and 24 years, on a face-to-face, lecturer and listener basis. Research has conventionally been viewed as the unfettered quest for understanding in the effort to expand the frontiers of disciplinary knowledge and has been funded primarily by the state. Community service has habitually taken the form of pro-bono education or social services by academic staff and students to the immediately surrounding community or to the nation.

The arrival of a globally competitive, knowledge-based economy is quickly reshaping these traditional understandings regarding the role of tertiary institutions. Rapid expansion of knowledge and technology has reduced the "use life" of knowledge, and created needs for worker retraining and lifelong learning, thus broadening the definition of "student" to encompass much of the adult population.[15] The widening availability of information and communication technologies means that knowledge can be acquired anywhere, and face-to-face learning becomes less of a requirement. Research takes on Mode 2 characteristics (Gibbons 1998), and is carried out within networked national innovation systems in which the state becomes merely a facilitator of funding.[16] Massification of tertiary enrollments and the rising costs of tertiary provision have generated pressures for lower-cost delivery systems, institutional income generation, and institutional accountability in terms of its direct contribution to national economic and social development. Even community service is being recast as a "third mission" (Bleiklie, Laredo, and Sorlin 2007; Laredo 2007; World Bank 2007) in which training, problem solving, and knowledge transfer in support of the economy become the reconstructed definition of service. In the process, the tertiary institution takes on a new service role as a "knowledge conglomerate" (Mohrman, Ma, and Baker 2008). In short, increasing societal welfare depends upon a nation's economic competitiveness, and upon its associated capacity to produce skilled workers and apply knowledge in order to meet this challenge. Let us therefore take stock of SSA's capacities to provide teaching, research, and third-mission service from this particular perspective.

Teaching

One dimension of teaching capacity is the quality of tertiary graduates across Sub-Saharan Africa. The general lack of empirical indicators makes this problem difficult to document. Nevertheless, a widespread belief persists that educational quality has fallen. This conclusion is indirectly supported by statistics on tertiary expenditures. Tertiary enrollments soared while government spending on tertiary education declined by 28 percent between 1980 and 2002 (World Bank EdStats 2008).[17] Consequently, expenditure per student was pushed down from US$6,800 in 1980 to US$1,200 in 2002 (Materu 2007). By 2004/2005, it averaged just US$981 in 33 low-income SSA countries (Mingat 2008).[18] It is difficult to imagine anything other than an erosion of educational quality under these conditions.[19]

Our country surveys reaffirmed the strong impression conveyed by casual empiricism that the principal contribution of universities to the knowledge economy in the seven countries is through the education of students, the traditional role of universities.[20] That standards have been slipping was evident, for example, in the responses from firms in Ghana, Kenya, and Mauritius, which expressed strong reservations about the quality of graduates. The problem of quality is being exacerbated by the rapid expansion of tertiary education without a corresponding increase in resources to universities to accommodate such an increase (See table 2.4). This has resulted in higher student-teacher ratios and lower expenditures per student.[21] In addition, training of future faculty members is not keeping pace. Furthermore, equipment used at universities in places like Kenya and Nigeria tends to be outdated, and has often been retired by local firms. The average age of laboratory equipment was reported to be 12 years for basic sciences and 16 years for engineering (African Network of Scientific and Technological Institutions 2005). This deficiency in resources (coupled with brain drain and low salaries of faculty) is a severe constraint on teaching and research at universities.[22]

Table 2.4   Changes in Public Expenditures on Education in Low-income Countries, 1990-2003

| | Current expenditure on education | | | |
| | As percent of government resources | | As percent of GDP | |
Region	early 1990s	around 2003	early 1990s	around 2003
Africa	19.3	18.2	3.1	3.3
Francophone	22.9	17.6	3.3	2.7
Anglophone	16.1	21.4	3.0	4.5
Other	12.9	11.7	2.4	2.0
Outside Africa	21.9	18.7	4.0	3.0
As a whole	19.9	18.3	3.4	3.2

Source: World Bank 2008c.

The academic staffing crisis. Perhaps the hardest task of all will be the recruiting of faculty and researchers to shoulder the rapidly expanding task of imparting education to rising numbers of students, and conducting research, some of it for the purposes of commercialization. In Francophone countries alone, meeting the projected increase in enrollment while keeping the student-teacher ratio constant will require 58,000 additional lecturers to be hired between 2006 and 2015, which is twice as many teachers who trained from 1970 to 2005 (World Bank 2008d).

A combination of inadequate salaries, heavy teaching workloads produced by low staff-student ratios,[23] deficient personnel management, and lack of research opportunities make staff retention and recruitment difficult (Mihyo 2008). Brain drain among university graduates in Sub-Saharan Africa is estimated at nearly one-third (Docquier and Marfouk 2005). AIDS exacts an unknown toll, and an aging professoriate compounds the problem of teacher supply for expanding systems.[24] Half of South African University faculty, 43 percent of academic staff at the University of Nairobi, and 50 percent of academic staff at the University of Ghana are over 50 years of age and nearing retirement. Many African countries have a mandatory retirement age at public universities (Mouton 2008; Tettey 2006).[25] In Ethiopia, staff shortages are reportedly forcing the use of graduates with bachelor's degrees to teach undergraduates following the recent tripling in the number of public universities.

As a result of these dynamics, vacancy rates in university staff positions frequently run between 25 percent and 50 percent. The University of Botswana had 465 vacancies that it could not fill in 2006–07 (Azcona and others 2008). In a survey of 20 universities conducted in 2003, an average staff vacancy rate in basic science departments of 31 percent was recorded (African Network of Scientific and Technical Institutions 2005). Vacancies are most prevalent in the fields of engineering, science, and business administration—the same disciplines most commonly associated with innovation and growth. For example, the African Network of Scientific and Technological Institutions (ANSTI) survey found staff vacancy rates of 37 percent for mathematics, 38 percent for biochemistry, and 41 percent for computer science. Nor is this a new problem. In Nigeria, a systemwide vacancy rate for university staff of 52 percent was reported in 1999 (National Universities Commission 2002).

New doctoral students are not coming out of graduate schools fast enough to replace retiring faculty members, let alone increase the number of faculty members with doctorates (Ng'ethe and Ngome 2007). For example, only 15 percent of university staff in Mozambique hold a doctoral degree. At Jomo Kenyatta University of Agriculture and Technology (Kenya) and Makerere University (Uganda), this share is 30 percent. In Ethiopia, academic personnel with doctorate degrees decreased from 28 percent in 1995–96 to 9 percent in 2002–03. This clearly suggests a need to increase graduate output from master's and PhD programs, especially in science and technology fields.

Research

Universities in Africa do not yet possess the research capabilities needed to combine global knowledge with national experience in support of innovation and problem solving. But this is not to say that they are lacking in capacity. In fact, academic researchers representing a range of disciplines across the continent have contributed regularly, albeit modestly, to internationally refereed academic journals, a main criterion for academic advancement (Sawyerr 2004). Rather, the prevailing incentive system for research in most universities does not encourage applied inquiry or problem-based collaboration with business, industry, or nongovernmental partners, as has been aggressively promoted in Korea (Sonu 2007) and Singapore (Lee and Win 2004). In addition, difficult budget choices during a 20-year period of soaring enrollments and falling per-student expenditures have typically favored teaching over research, as would be expected, but as a consequence have weakened the knowledge infrastructure that supports scientific investigation, e.g., scientific journals, books, research equipment, staff development, communications, and conference attendance (African Network of Scientific and Technological Institutions 2005; Sawyerr 2004).

Measuring the number of researchers per million inhabitants is a common way of comparing the human resource base for research among countries. Table 2.5 indicates a sizable R&D human resource gap between African nations and some of their economic competitors. This gap results from an interplay of supply and demand factors, including weak postgraduate output, brain drain, and attrition caused by retirements and HIV/AIDS deaths. Research skills are most commonly acquired during PhD training, but African PhD output has been sparse. The secretary general of the Association of African Universities reports, "The extreme weakness of graduate study programs in most African universities is among the most serious of the institutional limitations on research capacity development" (Sawyerr 2004). For example, the Ghanaian higher education system hosted just 127 PhD students within

Table 2.5   Researchers per Million Persons

Case study countries	Researchers per million population[a]	Comparators	Researchers per million population[a]
Ghana	n.a.	Sub-Saharan Africa	48
Kenya	n.a.	North Africa	160
Mauritius	201	Latin America	261
Nigeria	15	Brazil	168
South Africa	192	India	158
Tanzania	n.a.	China	459
Uganda	25	United States	4,103

Sources: World Development Indicators 2005; UNESCO Science Report 2005; Mouton 2008.
a. Data from various dates, 1996–2002.

its 111 postgraduate programs in 2002 (Gyekye 2002). In Ethiopia, just 28 PhD students were enrolled in 2004, and only a single PhD degree was awarded within this nation of 71 million inhabitants (Ministry of Education of Ethiopia 2005).

Africa's research output within the university world, as traditionally measured by scientific publications in international peer-reviewed journals, is meager (see tables 2.6 and 2.7). South Africa and Egypt together account for half of Africa's scientific publications. An additional 25 percent are generated by Kenya, Morocco, Nigeria, and Tunisia. The dominant themes of these publications are medicine and agriculture (Gaillard and Waast 2001, cited in Shabani 2006).[26] The region's research is largely of three types: academically oriented research in universities; consultancies for international organizations; and mission-oriented research undertaken mainly in international agencies (e.g., World Health Organization, Consultative Group on International Agricultural Research), but occasionally in government-based laboratories (Mouton 2008).

By the end of the twentieth century, funding for research in Africa had become the unintended victim of educational expansion and other competing budgetary demands such as health care, infrastructure development, and urban services. In 2000, Africa devoted just 0.3 percent of its gross domestic product (GDP) to research and development,[27] and contributed only 0.5 percent of the world's total R&D investments (Solimano 2002, cited in Tettey 2006). In terms of R&D expenditures as a percentage of GDP, Uganda and South Africa invest the most, at 0.82 and 0.68 percent, respectively, compared to 0.8 percent in India, 1.2 percent in China, and 2.5 percent in Korea (World Development Indictors 2005).

Table 2.6   Research Outputs by Geographical Region

Region	Scientific publications (2005)	Patent applications filed by residents (2004)
East Asia and Pacific	44,064	66,931
Europe and Central Asia	39,975	34,121
Latin America and Caribbean	20,045	4,890
Middle East and North Africa	6,354	486
South Asia	15,429	6,795
Sub-Saharan Africa	3,563	16

Source: World Development Indicators.

Table 2.7   Science and Engineering Publications from Africa, 2005–06

Country	Share of world output (%)
South Africa	0.37
Egypt	0.26
Tunisia	0.11
Morocco	0.09
Nigeria	0.08
Algeria	0.08
Kenya	0.05
Cameroon	0.03
Tanzania	0.03
Ethiopia	0.03
Uganda	0.02
Ghana	0.02
Senegal	0.02
Zimbabwe	0.02
Rest of Africa (39 countries)	0.16
Total Africa	1.37

Source: Hassan 2007.

Quantitatively, South Africa alone accounted for nearly two-thirds of the region's R&D expenditures (Sambo 2005).

Because agriculture is a large part of the regional economy, SSA capacities for agricultural research deserve a closer look. Agricultural R&D grew rapidly in the 1960s but then slowed, and during the 30-year period after 1971, it increased by just 1.4 percent per annum (Beintema and Stads 2006). By 2000, it amounted to US$1.5 billion in purchasing power parity terms and US$508 million in 1993 U.S. dollars, with almost 40 percent of the spending concentrated in South Africa and Nigeria (see figure 2.9). By 2000, Africa was spending US$0.70 on agriculture

Figure 2.9   Total Public Agricultural Research Spending in Sub-Saharan Africa, 2000

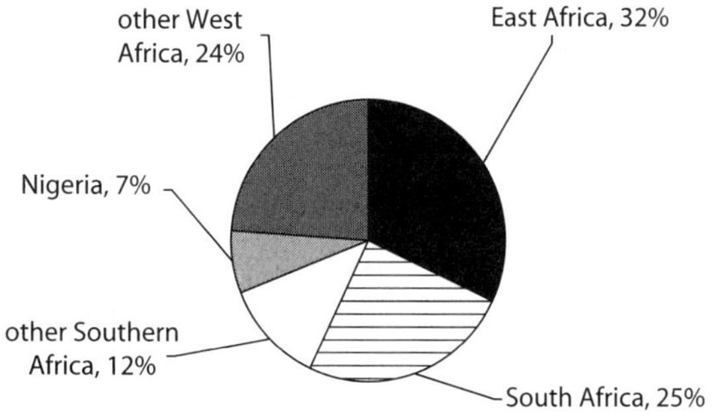

other West Africa, 24%

East Africa, 32%

Nigeria, 7%

other Southern Africa, 12%

South Africa, 25%

Source: Beintema and Stads (2006).

R&D from every US$100 of agricultural output, and the region as a whole employed just 12,000 researchers. Moreover, the average expenditure per researcher in 2000—approximately US$100,000 in constant 1993 dollars—was one-third less than what it was in 1980.[28] The problem is compounded by the small number of researchers, with half of all the countries employing less than 100, and little agricultural research being conducted in the universities. International research programs spearheaded by the Consultative Group on International Agricultural Research (CGIAR), the French Agricultural Research Centre for International Development (CIRAD), and International Relief & Development (IRD) provide much needed supplements to domestic research activities, but the combined national and international spending remains too low, and the international funds have not offset the stagnation of public spending in SSA countries.

The principal providers of funding for university research are foreign donor organizations. At the University of Ouagadougou in Burkina Faso, 90 percent of research is funded by donors (Shabani 2006). In Tanzania, more than half of all research is underwritten by donors. University research in Ethiopia is reportedly financed largely by donors (Wondimu 2003). While donor funding for research is certainly beneficial, it tends to be heavily concentrated on health problems, poverty analysis, environmental resources, education, women's issues, and other topics with a "public goods" orientation. Very little donor-funded research is oriented toward economic growth, competitiveness concerns, and agricultural technologies.[29] Consequently, were national research capabilities to be augmented, they could contribute significantly to Africa's new "growth agenda."

Third-Mission Service

Tertiary institutions in SSA, more so in some countries than in others, have been slow to engage in the new "third mission" that calls on them to become more actively integrated actors within the emerging national innovation systems catalyzed by twenty-first century globalization. A long-standing contribution by tertiary institutions to growing the economies of their countries is the provision of technical assistance in the form of con-sultancies. Indeed, faculty members engage in consulting in all of the seven countries surveyed. These consultancies tend to be informal, although some universities are encouraging formal consulting so as to obtain a share of the income. For example, the engineering department at the Kwame Nkrumah University of Science and Technology in Ghana has established the Technology Consultancy Center. While this may con-tribute to local economic development and university budgets, there is a risk that the time allocation of science and engineering faculties may become too slanted toward consulting and away from teaching and research (Essegbey 2007).

New ways of supporting economic growth are appearing. For example, universities are setting up technology licensing offices to market their inventions. In Kenya, Jomo Kenyatta University of Agriculture and Technology has 26 patents and they are managed by Jomo Kenyatta University of Agriculture and Technology Enterprise Ltd. However, so far, only a few patents have been licensed and even fewer have yielded com-mercial results (Ng'ethe and Ngome 2007). Some universities, as in Ghana, do not have any patents yet (Essegbey 2007). In other countries such as Tanzania, intermediary organizations based in universities are offering net-working and exhibition opportunities to better inform the private sector of the availability of technologies and research conducted at universities.[30]

Some tertiary institutions are supplementing their revenues by offering courses customized for the needs of industry. For example, in Kenya, Jomo Kenyatta University and Maseno University offer courses in flori-culture that assist the cut flower cluster near Lake Naivasha meet its technical needs (Zeng 2008). Universities in Kenya, Mauritius, Tanzania, and Uganda are requiring students to undertake internships with busi-nesses so that students will have exposure to real world issues (Bunwaree and Sobhee 2007; Kaijage 2007; Ng'ethe and Ngome 2007; Tusubira and Ndiwalana 2007). In this manner, students can also serve as agents trans-mitting practical knowledge and the requirements of industry back to universities, making it possible for faculties to adjust their curricula based on this feedback.

In a few instances, universities are filling voids in the marketplace by producing capital goods of a low-tech variety. For instance, the Technology Consultancy Center at the Kwame Nkrumah University of Science and Technology produces beekeeping and other equipment (Essegbey 2007). Jomo Kenyatta University of Agriculture and Technology developed and produced equipment to make lantern parts for local small businesses and a fresh juice making machine for street vendors. Others are developing software packages needed by businesses, such as the accounting and estate management software developed by Jomo Kenyatta University of Agriculture and Technology (Ng'ethe and Ngome 2007). In other countries, these software packages would be supplied by private firms, but because such providers are absent, the university has stepped into the breach.

Other successful cases of linkages are between universities and agro-industries, such as the wine industry in South Africa. There are three reasons for these, arising from the nature of agriculture. In several countries, agriculture is the dominant production sector. For instance, agriculture accounts for half of GDP, two-thirds of exports, and 80 percent of employment in Tanzania. Second, the knowledge needed by farmers comes both from international and local sources. Knowledge from abroad is vital to the efficient cultivation of many agricultural commodities, but frequently needs to be adapted to local conditions. Finally, the problems facing farmers tend to be industrywide concerns, such as diseases and pests. The solution benefits the farmers in general, and if there is an organization that can aggregate the demand from individual farmers effectively, they can collectively seek solutions to the industrywide problem, such as the Wine Industry Network of Expertise and Technology (Winetech) in South Africa has done. Winetech mobilizes scientists and technicians to advise the wine cluster by drawing upon universities and the specialized institute for viticulture and oenology created by the Agriculture Research Council, which is partially state funded (Wood and Kaplan, in Zeng 2008).[31]

For manufacturers, the problems they face are frequently specific to individual firms. In such instances, an aggregation of demand from industry may be difficult, and collaboration between universities and firms depends on initiatives by firms and universities together. While this may work for larger firms, which are often engaged in in-house research activities and search widely for solutions to their particular problems, smaller firms tend to find it difficult to identify suitable universities or faculties and researchers that can assist them.[32]

This is reflected in various published case studies examining university-industry linkages. Larger local firms tend to collaborate more with universities. The subsidiaries of foreign firms tend to rely on their own intrafirm sources of technology for much of their needs. Hence, if the economy is dominated by large multinational corporations, the demand for university-industry linkages can be less than if the economy is populated by local firms. However, even in the case of local firms, it is not only size that matters, but the absorptive capacity of the firm and its orientation toward exports. Firms regularly engaging in innovation activities are more likely to seek linkages with universities. Firms that export also tend to collaborate more with universities.

For many firms in Africa, the main source of technology is embedded in the equipment purchased, mainly from abroad (see figure 2.10).[33] While some firms are able to modify this equipment, many opt to

Figure 2.10   Source of Technology for Firms in Sub-Saharan Africa

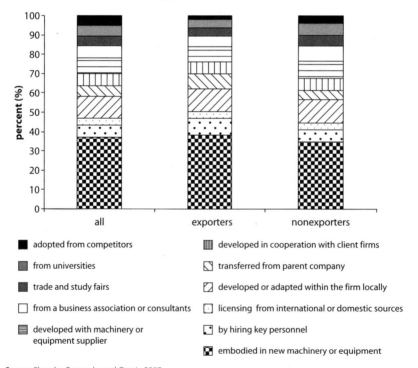

Source: Chandra, Boccardo, and Osorio 2007.

purchase a "newer" vintage if firm executives believe they need to upgrade technology.[34] For instance, in Mauritius, only about one-third of firms modify equipment, while the others tend to merely purchase new equipment. Local innovation in the clothing industry is rare, even though Mauritius is better supplied with skills and research capacity than many other African countries and badly needs to upgrade its products and processes to compete with other countries (Zeng 2008). Even firms willing to tinker with equipment often face difficulties in securing necessary parts and components to make adjustments. Recently, firms in Ghana, Kenya, Mauritius, South Africa, and Uganda have begun to use the Internet to gather information on industrial technologies, which is a promising shift in attitudes toward improving competitiveness.

For the purposes of industrial development, the economies in Africa tend to lack many of the complementary activities that are necessary for local firms to grow. While some economies see a large number of new "firm" start-ups, they tend to be located in the informal sector. Without access to additional risk capital or other institutions and incentives for the local sourcing of parts and components—common through East Asia—these firms remain informal and small. Such firms tend not to engage in innovation activities, or to export. And their demand for services offered by universities remains minimal, including the demand for graduates.

Universities are adjusting to their emerging "third mission" by encouraging internships and consultancies to better respond to the demand from industries. However, universities cannot neglect their other traditional roles of teaching and research. But at least some of the universities should be able to provide both quality education and research. In some cases, new courses may need to be added, such as on quality and environment management (ISO 9001 and 14000), which are adopted by firms (for instance in Kenya). These courses are necessary, especially for exporting firms that must adhere to international standards. Universities also must possess good applied research capability, which could help spawn links with local industry. For instance, boat-making firms in South Africa are unable to collaborate with local universities because local universities do not have any specific programs and research in the area of boat making (such as advanced materials specific to boats). As a result, they collaborate with universities in the United States (Kruss and Lorentzen 2007). Firms in this study reported that they still rely on workshops and seminars organized by local universities to get an idea of what kind of technologies are available.[35]

Africa also lacks intermediary organizations that in other countries have served as matchmakers between researchers and users of technologies. Intermediaries have helped to develop or adapt technologies so as to make them commercially viable, have pooled lab facilities so that firms can access equipment they would not be able to afford, and mobilized resources for start-ups, for scholarships, for specific research projects, and to fund incubators (Howells 2006; Yusuf 2008). The technology transfer offices in universities are one type of intermediary. Others include the Technology Advanced Metropolitan Area (TAMA) association in Japan (Kodama 2008), Fraunhofer Institutes in Germany, Spinno/Tekes in Finland, and the Technology Transfer from Research Institute to SMEs (TEFT) program in Norway. India created the Council of Scientific and Industrial Research, which is an independent body under the prime minister that is tasked with promoting research in areas with commercial promise, building R&D capabilities, and disseminating research findings (World Bank Institute 2007). The Fundacion Chile has achieved fame in Latin America through its successful efforts to start up innovative enterprises in association with the private sector, assist them in accessing and adapting technologies, and more broadly, helped to create an infrastructure for the acquisition and transfer of technologies. Other examples include the Malaysian Agricultural Research and Development Institute, which works with the Malaysian Palm Oil Board and the universities to develop new products based on Malaysia's major tree crops (Rasiah 2006). In the African context, the scale of the activities in any one country argues for regional operations embracing universities in several contiguous countries. Technology development funds, which have been utilized by Latin American countries, can also reinforce the activities of intermediaries. However, the effectiveness of these funds for promoting technology development is not convincingly validated (Hall and Maffioli 2008).

Even if tertiary institutions are willing to collaborate with industries, if firms are not interested in innovation activities, then successful partnerships will not materialize. In general, firms are not spending much on innovation activities in Africa. In Mauritius, the R&D spending is only 0.3 percent of GDP. This modest effort clearly needs to increase. But it is likely to only when firms take the lead in developing more research-intensive activities, and seek new technology so as to enter more promising markets.

Notes

1. See, for example, recent policy statements on this topic by Australia (DEST 2003), Denmark (Ministry of Education 2004), and the United Kingdom (DfES 2004).

2. The experience of the past four decades has also deepened our understanding of the market for skills. It has proven difficult to predict the demand for specific skills 10 and 15 years into the future, and hence, detailed long-term manpower planning delinked from specific projected employer demand is of limited value. Many governments embraced manpower planning during the 1950s and 1960s to varying degrees. The socialist economies clung on to this practice for much longer, only relinquishing it gradually once the rigidities and imbalances it introduced had become glaringly apparent, and the countries had commenced the transition to market economies. Nevertheless, it is also apparent that education ministries and educators need to anticipate the demand for broad skill categories and to equip, finance, and orient the education system to approximately meet these longer-term demands. Moreover, when industrial trends are clearly pointing to the need for particular skills over the near term, taking steps to increase the responsiveness of supply makes sound policy sense.

3. On average, the demand for higher education in Francophone countries will be 2.5 times the current enrollment, although the estimates vary widely from country to country. The highest, Djibouti, will be faced with 13,000 incoming students in 2015, 12 times the current enrollment if the trends persist (World Bank 2008c). One forecast puts the budget shortfall at US$3 billion for a group of 18 Francophone countries for the period between 2006–15. This is based on the unit cost of a student of US$3,600, which would add up to US$4 billion in additional investment needs. The current budget allocation of US$80 million per year for all the Francophone countries, and assuming 5 percent annual growth, would yield only US$1 billion, resulting in a US$3 billion shortfall (World Bank 2008d).

4. Publicly provided funds finance 90 percent of the operational expenses of tertiary educational institutions, especially universities. Enrollment fees have not changed in the last 15 years for many of the Francophone countries. Budgets allocated to education range from 15 percent to 30 percent of a country's total budget in Francophone countries (the average is 21 percent). Within the education budget, the share for tertiary education ranges from 15 percent to 30 percent, with an average of 20 percent (World Bank 2008d).

5. For instance, Côte d'Ivoire was successful in promoting private universities, and after seven years in operation, 30 percent of students are enrolled at private institutions (World Bank 2008d).

6. In Francophone countries, more than 45 percent of the budget earmarked for higher education is used for student assistance in the form of scholarships, food, housing, transport, etc. (World Bank 2008d).

7. From a political perspective, it is said that tertiary enrollment expansion has many godfathers, whereas quality is usually an orphan.

8. Whereas 16 percent of public employees possess tertiary education, just 8 percent of modern private sector employees do (Mingat and Majgaard 2008).

9. Carried out by local university research teams supervised by the Centre for Research on Higher Education and Work of the University of Kassel, Germany and by the Association of African Universities (Mugabushaka, Schomburg, and Teichler 2007).

10. African tertiary institutions are beginning to utilize employer surveys and graduate tracer studies to good effect in guiding curriculum reform. If resources permit, these can be carried out every five years to identify changing skill requirements in the labor market. In Tanzania, Sokoine University of Agriculture surveyed its graduates and their employers in 2004 for feedback on graduate performance in employment (Afrozone 2005; Agrisystems [Eastern Africa] 2005; Development Associates 2005; K-Rep Advisory Services 2005). Likewise, the University of Dar es Salaam, prompted by concerns raised in an academic audit conducted in 1998, undertook its first-ever tracer study between 2002 and 2003 as part of its institutional transformation program. The study covered all the academic units in the university, and its findings served as a key input to curriculum updating. According to the university, "tracer studies have a positive effect on the institution's ability to remain competitive among the many providers of education, training and/or learning opportunities" (Mkude and Ishumi 2004). Regular curriculum reviews by panels comprised of employer representatives and subject matter specialists (including some from other tertiary institutions and perhaps even from overseas) are another means of ensuring that graduate output responds to labor market demands.

11. It also conceals considerable differences among individual countries. For example, the Central African Republic, Chad, Democratic Republic of Congo, Malawi, Mozambique, Niger, and Tanzania have gross enrollment rates of around 1 percent, whereas Mauritius, Nigeria, and South Africa have gross enrollment rates of 10 percent to 15 percent, which are nearing the world average.

12. Declining shares of S&T enrollments have also been recorded in a majority of OECD countries (OECD 2006).

13. For a fuller discussion of the development of private higher education in Africa, see Varghese (2008).

14. Mingat and Majgaard (2008, p. 55) report that private tertiary enrollments account for 18 percent of the total in 33 low-income SSA countries.

15. In recognition of this reality, the government of Rwanda has defined the standard work day as 7:00 a.m. to 3:30 p.m. so that its citizens will be able to further their education in the evening.

16. Governments play this facilitating role by providing incentives to encourage partnerships between research universities and corporate enterprises. The term "triple helix" is sometimes used to refer to this new relationship among university, industry, and government (Etzkowitz and Leydesdorff 1998).

17. In comparison, all other regions except Latin America have increased their share of tertiary education spending within their total education spending.

18. The average unit expenditure for tertiary education in SSA middle-income countries was US$2,554.

19. As a result of the recent decline in the value of the U.S. dollar, unit costs for SSA tertiary education may have risen in recent years if expressed in terms of U.S. dollars. However, this should not necessarily suggest any corresponding improvement in educational quality.

20. For example, some 60 percent of the owners of small businesses at the Otigba computer cluster in Lagos, Nigeria, have a university-level education, but formal research-related links with universities are few. While the Kamukunji engineering and repair cluster in Nairobi, Kenya, could use research and skills, it also has little contact with nearby universities (Zeng 2008).

21. Student-teacher ratios as high as 133:1 for physics, 120:1 for mathematics, and 93:1 for computer science were found in 2003 (ANSTI 2005b, p. 29). While a large number of studies examine class size at primary and secondary levels, and its effects on student performance, relatively little research has been conducted for tertiary education. Kokkelenberg, Dillon, and Christy (2008) find that class size indeed matters for student performance. The inflection point seems to be a class size of 20. There is a steep decline in student performance when moving from a small class to a class size of 20. However, once a class becomes larger than 20 students, the negative impact of the increase in class sizes is muted.

22. The starting salary of a lecturer is US$600 in Mauritius and US$772 in Ghana. Notably, some have argued that brain drain is not simply a function of low salaries, and that institutions could do much to retain staff by improving the fairness and transparency of personnel and administrative decisions within the work environment (Mihyo 2008; Tettey 2006).

23. For example, staff-student ratios for West African universities increased from 1:14 in 1990 to 1:32 in 2002 (UIS/UNESCO 2005). In some countries, such as Madagascar, teaching loads are low because of inefficient pedagogical practices.

24. For an informative reference on emerging good practices with regard to HIV/AIDS within African tertiary institutions, see Association of African Universities (2007), available at: www.aau.org/aur-hiv-aids/docs/AAUBP-report.pdf.

25. The challenge of replacing aging faculty is not unique to Africa. One out of three academic staff in France and one out of five staff in Australia, Belgium, and Sweden are over 55 years of age (Kaiser, Hillegers, and Legro 2005, p. 65).

26. "Due to inadequate funding, poor management of research funds, lack of research infrastructure, and the inability of universities to develop links with industry, Nigerian universities produce a preponderance of basic research that can be published but may not contribute directly to economic growth or productivity" (Ng'ethe, Subotzky, and Afeti 2006, p. 62).

27. In contrast, the OECD average is 2 percent to 3 percent (World Bank 2006, p. 29). In the quest to increase their competitiveness in the global knowledge economy, the governments of Denmark and Malaysia have recently announced their intentions to double the share of GDP that they spend on R&D.

28. The decline of agricultural science was exacerbated by cutbacks in external assistance during the 1980s and 1990s (Paarlberg 2008). From a peak of 18 percent of foreign assistance in 1979, development assistance for agricultural research and infrastructure fell below 3 percent in 2005 to US$3 billion. The result has been declining growth in agricultural productivity and a heavy reliance on energy inputs (*Financial Times* 2008).

29. The long-term neglect of agricultural R&D and the unwillingness of most African countries to explore the potential of genetically modified technologies, especially for drought-resistant crops, affects food security and longer-term export prospects (Paarlberg 2008). Worldwide, 29 countries plant genetically modified crops, particularly, corn, soya, and cotton, and they account for 8 percent of planted acreage (*Oxford Analytica* 2008b).

30. In the case of Tanzania, the Tanzania Commission for Universities organizes the exhibition.

31. The shrimp industry in Thailand benefited from successful links with a local university (Brimble and Doner 2007). The education levels of farmers are no less important for new technologies to be assimilated (Weir and Knight 2007; Foster and Rosenzweig 1996).

32. In such cases, the solution may lie in the creation of "consolidated services organizations" that provide R&D, technology transfer, and technical assistance services for a grouping of smaller firms within a specific industrial subsector, as is done for plastics and rubber manufacturing in Colombia (Noriega 2007).

33. Investment Climate Surveys on SSA countries find that the purchase of machinery is an important source of new technology. Almost 30 percent of firms obtained new technology through the purchase of a production machine or equipment from suppliers. An additional 10 percent acquired new technology by developing or adapting existing technologies within the firm. An international study of technology acquisition in developing countries identified 12 different ways that firms access technology. The primary means was through new equipment purchase; university collaboration was ranked last (Gore 2007).

34. "Newer" means that the equipment may be secondhand or an older model, but "new" for the domestic firm.

35. Firms also increasingly rely on the Internet to keep themselves up-to-date on developments in their industries.

CHAPTER 3

Improving the Performance of Tertiary Education in Sub-Saharan Africa

Introducing National Innovation Systems

The global knowledge economy has drawn attention to the value of "national innovation systems" in the competition among nations (Nelson 1993; Porter 1990; Stern, Porter, and Furman 2000; Thurow 1999; World Bank 1999). Institutions that generate skills and knowledge, such as universities and research institutes, are essential components of a national innovation system (NIS). In essence, an NIS is a melding of institutional capacities, coordination mechanisms, communication networks, and policy incentives that fosters innovation-led gains in economic productivity. In this web of institutional relationships, innovation can arise at any point. Knowledge is no longer the disciplinary monopoly of a few institutions of higher learning; rather, it is becoming the product of transdisciplinary problem-solving endeavors conducted within a shifting network of often informal professional interactions (Gibbons and others 1994; Gibbons 1998).[1]

NIS analysis emphasizes the need to understand key organizational actors from different economic and social sectors, their organizational behaviors, and the institutional context within which they interact. This in turn draws policy attention to institutional structures of governance and management (for greater flexibility and responsiveness), criteria and incentives for professional performance (for improved productivity), and access to information and interinstitutional communication networks (for enhanced competitiveness).

The result is a growing strategic interest in the development of "core competencies" in business, science, technology, and applied research.[2] As noted earlier, this is often accompanied by efforts to reformulate the traditional community service expectation of tertiary institutions into a stronger "third mission" that seeks mutually beneficial collaboration with the private sector (Bleiklie and Kogan 2007; Laredo 2007). In these circumstances, the challenge for educational systems is not simply to introduce appropriate reforms, but to create an environment of continuous reform in which innovation and adaptation become permanent features. Nations as diverse as Australia, Chile, Malaysia, and Spain have responded by developing cross-sectoral policy frameworks to promote science, technology, and innovation.[3] Within Sub-Saharan Africa, Mozambique, Rwanda, and South Africa have led the way with similar cross-cutting strategies.[4] Other SSA countries that have produced national science and technology policies since 2000 include Ethiopia, Ghana, Lesotho, Malawi, Senegal, Tanzania, Uganda, Zambia, and Zimbabwe (Mouton 2008).[5]

During the past decade, most African countries have pursued national economic growth strategies within the framework of Poverty Reduction Strategy Papers (PRSPs). Until recently, many PRSPs have been oriented toward attainment of the Millennium Development Goals, an internationally accepted set of performance targets spanning poverty alleviation, agriculture, and access to basic services. Concern with explicit growth promotion efforts as the means for sustainable poverty reduction is a relatively recent—but readily accepted—shift of strategic approach (Commission for Africa 2005).

A comparative reading of recent African PRSPs from 2003–07 brings to light several common themes in proposed PRSP activities that have direct implications for the knowledge and skills needed to implement them successfully. Examples include the development of alternative energy sources, enhanced telecommunications and ICT capacities, increased agricultural output, expanded road construction and maintenance, natural resource management, and a continuing emphasis on maternal/child health and HIV/AIDS prevention and treatment. The missing link is to make these human capital requirements more explicit. One way to do this is through a national human resource development plan tied to a country's PRSP. A more detailed assessment of PRSPs from 14 African countries, which draws out the knowledge and skills implications of their stated goals, is provided in Annex B. All of this suggests the usefulness of more careful attention to matching the supply with the demand for tertiary graduates in Sub-Saharan Africa.

What Is the Current State of Play?

Tertiary education is an integral part of the larger education sector and shares in the responsibility, together with other levels of the education system, of meeting four pervasive sectorwide challenges. These are equity, access, quality, and financing.

Equity. Developing education systems contend with inequities at all levels. Inequities are particularly acute in tertiary education, where on average a student from the lowest socioeconomic quintile has 15 times less chance of entering a university than one from the highest quintile (Brossard and Foko 2007). In Chad, 92 percent of university students come from the top quintile (World Bank 2007b). In Burundi, the 2 percent of students who attain higher education are benefited by 40 percent of education sector expenditures (World Bank 2007a). In Lesotho, the top quintile of students receives 47 percent of the education budget (World Bank 2005). In Malawi, enrollment in tertiary education is associated almost exclusively with households from the richest 10 percent of the population (World Bank 2004a). Such statistics imply that some scope may remain for further efforts at cost sharing within tertiary education.

Access. Despite tripling tertiary enrollments over the past 15 years, the regional enrollment ratio for tertiary education currently stands at only 5 percent. Both secondary and tertiary enrollment ratios for SSA are the lowest among the eight major geographical regions of the world. Despite the recent gains achieved in expanding access at all educational levels, few Africans would argue that these enrollment levels are adequate for future development. As a result, the political pressure for continued expansion at all educational levels is fierce.

Quality. Various deficiencies produce poor-quality education at the secondary level, including outdated curricula, reduced time spent on instruction, shortages in textbooks, and underequipped specialized facilities. As a result, many students leave secondary school ill-prepared for tertiary education or for skill acquisition (World Bank 2008a). Tertiary education fares no better in terms of quality. Part of its curriculum is often dedicated to remedial efforts to make up for shortcomings at the lower levels of education. In a certain sense, the price to African education for its impressive enrollment expansion has been a loss of educational quality.

Financing. On average, SSA countries now spend 18.2 percent of government budgets and 4.5 percent of GDP on education. These are not insignificant shares, approaching and, in some cases, even surpassing the targets recommended by the Fast Track Initiative. These nations also devote an average of 20 percent of their education budgets to tertiary education, a proportion that borders on the high end of what is frequently accepted as good practice. At the same time, household surveys indicate that families are also making sizable financial contributions to the costs of educational provision, and the scope for increasing these further may be limited, particularly in light of globally rising food prices.[6] Consequently, the increased funding that will be needed in the future in order to address the above problems of educational access and quality will not be found easily. It is likely to require a combination of further efforts by governments and families, increased development assistance that maintains support to basic education while increasing funding for secondary and tertiary education, concerted efficiency gains at all levels, and some creative new delivery options as well—all within the context of continuing economic expansion.

Postsecondary Technical Education

Postsecondary technical education is a critical component of the tertiary education system. Technical education responds to an economic need: competence in the use of technologies or methods of organization employed by firms. In comparison with university education, it places technology ahead of science, and puts skills before knowledge. Its output is the "higher-level technician" who occupies the professional middle ground between the engineer and the highly skilled worker (Mazeran and others 2007).

The origins of postsecondary technical education are associated with the rise of more sophisticated industrial technologies in the late nineteenth century. Three different models of training emerged from these early experiences. One is the British "liberal" model, in which training content is negotiated between employers, workers' unions, and training providers based on market needs. A second is the French "centralized" model, in which the organization and content of training is set by government in consultation with employers and unions, and financed by employers on the basis of a specific tax. The third is the German "dual" model, in which training content is determined jointly by government, employers, and unions, and training includes alternating periods of work-based learning and classroom instruction (Mazeran and others 2007). The first two models have been dominant in SSA, although the German approach has garnered attention in recent years.

Technical education became institutionalized at the postsecondary level in the latter half of the twentieth century through polytechnics in Britain, University Institutes of Technology (UIT) in France, and *Fachhochschulen* in Germany.[7] They were joined by professional colleges in Canada, technical institutes in Japan, and community colleges in the United States. The UIT model proved attractive in various developing countries and was subsequently adopted by Brazil, Chile, Egypt, India, Korea, Mexico, Morocco, Tunisia, and Venezuela (Mazeran and others 2007).

During the late twentieth century, strong economic growth rates in a number of countries have been associated with effective technical education systems. Notable among them have been India, Ireland,[8] Korea, and Singapore. The Korean development model is often held up as an example in which technical education played a major role. In the 1960s, the Korean government pursued an aggressive economic development strategy in which junior colleges were important suppliers of skilled human resources. Both public and private technical education were encouraged. The government's role was to set firm rules on quality, provide incentives for collaboration with industry, and implement tailor-made courses to meet specific needs. In many cases, these training capacities were linked to the development of specific high-priority industries such as steel production and shipbuilding. Through technical education, the government was able to satisfy the economy's needs for skilled labor while reducing pressures on universities to enroll more students (UNESCO 2005).

In Sub-Saharan Africa, technical education dates largely from independence in the 1960s and 1970s, when the loss of expatriate skills provided by prior colonial administrations prompted the newly independent governments to establish state-sponsored education at all levels. These efforts were often guided by socialist principles, and manpower planning was commonly employed. Government ministries regularly included their own technical education training institutes that operated outside the purview of the education system.

This model was challenged by the World Bank in the late 1980s, initially in its comprehensive review of education in Sub-Saharan Africa (World Bank 1988), and subsequently in its global assessment of technical and vocational education (World Bank 1991b). The reports argued that considerable inefficiency was associated with costly, supply-driven technical training institutions, that they had poor links with the labor market, that many of their programs were judged ineffective, and that private providers were often constrained from entering the market.

Subsequently, World Bank assistance for technical and vocational education fell from an annual average of 22 percent of total education financing in SSA in the 1970s to only 5 percent per year in the 1990s (Johanson and Adams 2004). Although this decline was partly the consequence of the doubts registered above, it also reflected rising donor commitments to the Education for All and Millennium Development Goals campaigns.

Since the beginning of the twenty-first century, technical education has attracted growing policy attention as trade liberalization has required enterprises to draw on higher levels of skills in order to be competitive. Consequently, governments have increasingly expressed the need for high-level technicians and given renewed attention to technical education. In testimony to this change, the majority of current Poverty Reduction Strategy Papers in Sub-Saharan Africa mention technical education as an explicit part of their strategies. This is often provided through short-cycle programs (two years), which are less expensive than university education, and more accessible to disadvantaged and female students, both of which are underrepresented in the universities. For example, Senegal is in the process of creating regional university colleges (Collèges universitaries régionaux) to decentralize access to tertiary education and tie it more closely to regional economic growth strategies. Madagascar is undertaking a major reform and rationalization of its technical education system. Mauritania is set to open its first polytechnic-type institution (Institut supérieur d'enseignement polytechnique) in 2008. Mozambique has recently established three regional polytechnics and expects to set up two more.

At present, technical education in Sub-Saharan Africa seems ready to reassert itself. Numerous countries have undertaken reforms aimed at rectifying the shortcomings of earlier eras. The movement to provide institutions and managers with increased autonomy and accountability for results is improving the relevance and quality of skills development. Rigid centralized public systems have become more responsive where individual training institutions have been given the freedom to set fees, adapt training to local needs, hire appropriate staff, and choose methods of instruction. The shift in some countries from financing inputs to financing performance and outcomes has helped to create incentives for improvement (Johanson and Adams 2004). A major innovation is the move toward competency-based training, currently under way in Ghana, Madagascar, Mozambique, South Africa, Tanzania, and Zambia.[9]

Demand. Overall formal sector job growth in Africa, from either private or public sources, proved to be minimal during the economic stagnation of the 1990s. Employment creation in the private sector was miniscule or negative (with the exception of Botswana and Mauritius). Public sector job growth slowed or contracted with the structural adjustment reforms of the 1990s. Although the size of the labor force in SSA countries with a high prevalence of HIV/AIDS infection is projected to be between 10 percent and 30 percent smaller by 2020 than it would have been without AIDS (Johanson and Adams 2004), the continent's youth population is nevertheless expected to continue its strong growth for the foreseeable future, suggesting that the formal sector will not be able to generate jobs fast enough to absorb all labor market entrants (World Bank Institute 2007).

Under conditions of slow economic growth, competition for jobs can be fierce. The limited information available suggests that postsecondary technical graduates often compete well with university graduates for these jobs. In Nigeria, for example, the unemployment rate among polytechnic graduates was generally less than that for university graduates (World Bank 2006). Yet despite this positive showing, far greater social status is attached to the universities than to the technical institutes or polytechnics.

Supply. Some observers have noted that the nonuniversity sector seems to be expanding more quickly than the university sector (Varghese 2008; Ng'ethe, Subotzky, and Afeti 2007). Others indicate that the university sector lags only slightly (Mazeran and others 2007). This dynamism is likely due to the fact that many nonuniversity institutions offer short-duration and employment-oriented courses. Enrollments in shorter-cycle, technical education courses account for one-third or more of tertiary enrollments in 14 of 26 African countries for which there are data (table 3.1). Notably, SSA has a relatively high percentage of students enrolled in technical programs compared to other regions.

Costs. Technical education is expensive—as much as six times as costly as general secondary education and often on par with tertiary education (see table 3.2). In comparison with state-sponsored or privately provided technical education, enterprise-based training tends to be more effective. However, all three forms can be cost-effective when linked closely to employer demand and available jobs. But diversified secondary education, in which some occupational skills are included within an otherwise academic curriculum, has not proven to be cost-effective. It is an expensive form of secondary education because of the need for special facilities, equipment, and teachers, and it does not give graduates any proven advantage in the labor market (Johanson and Adams 2004).

Table 3.1   Percentage Distribution of Tertiary Students by Program Type, 2004

Country	Non-university education (ISCED 5B)	University education (ISCED 5A)
Botswana	19	81
Burundi	67	33
Comoros	32	68
Congo, Republic of	15	85
Eritrea	23	77
Ethiopia	0	100
Ghana	33	67
Kenya	33	67
Lesotho	49	51
Liberia	37	63
Madagascar	18	82
Malawi	0	100
Mali	5	95
Mauritania	5	95
Mauritius	57	43
Mozambique	0	100
Namibia	39	61
Nigeria	41	59
Rwanda	35	65
Sierra Leone	56	44
South Africa	12	88
Swaziland	0	100
Tanzania	20	80
Uganda	36	64
Zambia	41	59
Zimbabwe	59	38

Source: Global Education Digest 2006, UIS/UNESCO (http://www.uis.unesco.org/).
Note: Based on the UNESCO International Standard Classification of Education (ISCED) categories.

Financing. Five main sources for funding technical education can be identified. They are: payroll levies on employers; tuition and other fees paid by enterprises or trainees; production and sale of goods and services by training institutions; community support and donations; and, indirectly, the expansion of nongovernmental provision. Training levies are used in 12 SSA countries, but they are not without problems. These include employer noncompliance, diversion of resources to nontraining uses, and the potential for misuse of funds when surpluses are generated. Student fees have been steadily expanding and now underwrite roughly

Table 3.2   Unit Cost in U.S. Dollars of Secondary, Technical, and Tertiary Education, Selected Countries, 2002

Country	Upper secondary	Technical/ vocational	Tertiary
Benin	278	386	612
Burkina Faso	291	NA	1,364
Cameroon	354	583	484
Chad	157	896	926
Côte d'Ivoire	617	951	978
Ethiopia	59	355	636
Ghana	165	340	900
Madagascar	141	183	491
Mali	265	NA	481
Mauritania	139	771	538
Mozambique	145	180	1,535
Niger	309	NA	968
Nigeria	162	433	1,260
Senegal	460	624	1,513
Togo	118	362	332
Zambia	97	NA	567

Sources: World Bank EdStats, Pole de Dakar, Johanson and Adams 2004; World Bank 2006, 2008a.
NA = Not available

one-quarter of recurrent costs in many cases. Sale of goods and services can be an important revenue supplement, as long as a good balance is maintained between instruction and production. An appropriate "good practice" target for this income source is 10 percent to 15 percent of the recurrent budget. Public-private partnerships are a largely untapped resource, although employer sponsorship of selected students is growing. Nongovernmental provision, including by religious, nonprofit and for-profit organizations, is expanding rapidly.

One of the main means for financing technical education is through training funds, which are found in 21 SSA countries. They disburse funds received from the government, from training levies on payrolls of 1 percent to 3 percent (see table 3.3), or donors. By procuring training for target groups on a competitive basis, they level the playing field for providers and encourage cost-effective delivery. Characteristics of effective training funds include: transparent rules for allocation; representative governance that includes workers and employers; capable management; effective targeting instruments; regular monitoring and evaluation of training results; and constant attention to financial sustainability (Johanson and Adams 2004).

Table 3.3   National Technical Training Levy Schemes in Selected SSA Countries

Country	Training levy as percent of payroll
Benin	2.0
Côte d'Ivoire	1.2
Congo, Dem. Rep. of	1.0
Kenya	Sectoral taxes
Malawi	Based on number of skilled workers
Mali	0.5
Mauritius	1.0
Nigeria	1.2
Senegal	3.0
South Africa	1.0
Tanzania	2.0
Togo	1.0
Zimbabwe	1.0

Source: Johanson and Adams 2004.

Identified problems. At this point, the following constraints on the development of technical education have been identified: low capacity in terms of student numbers; the uncertain status of technical education in the public's view; severe shortages of technologist-teachers (teachers with applied experience in the productive sector); courses that are often ill matched with technologies currently in use by firms; a general shortage of training opportunities, except in the service sectors (accounting, secretarial, information technology); lack of self-assessment within the institutions; significant underfunding in many cases; lack of donor support;[10] and the general absence of statistical data on the technical education subsector. But perhaps the biggest obstacle for the current development of SSA technical education systems as a whole is their widespread lack of linkages and engagement with employers, especially in the private sector. In many systems, technical and vocational education and training have a poor image, which discourages students from seeking places in these programs.

Institutional drift is a particular problem (Ng'ethe, Subotzky, and Afeti 2007). Polytechnics often succumb to an "academic drift" toward degree programs, in part because of the application of funding formulas that tend to favor universities over polytechnics. In Nigeria, polytechnics are agitating to award degrees. In Kenya, two of the nation's three polytechnics have recently been elevated to university/ college status. In Ghana, academic staff unions within the polytechnics demanded parity with the universities following the introduction of a Bachelor of Science degree in Technology. As noted above, the "academic drift" problem is not confined to Africa, and can also be found in several developed countries.

Remedies. A new policy agenda has arisen in SSA in response to the earlier sharp critique of state-sponsored technical and vocational education systems. The first stage is to ensure that supportive macro conditions exist—incentives for investment in human and physical capital; economic policies that foster economic growth and employment; and good-quality primary and secondary education systems that provide workers with the necessary cognitive foundation for skills training.

The second stage focuses on improving the effectiveness of publicly provided training by developing strong links and partnerships between training institutions and enterprises, improving institutional responses to market forces, using resources more efficiently, building a capacity for technical and vocational education policy implementation, and diversifying sources of funding through payroll levies and cost recovery. It also focuses on improving privately provided training by creating an encouraging policy environment, providing incentives for employer-based training, and reducing the regulation of private training that is unrelated to quality assurance. It calls for reduced public involvement in direct provision, partnerships in governance, increased reliance on market mechanisms to ensure relevance, and improved efficiency. Reforms center on training levies, greater attention to the informal sector, developing entrepreneurship skills for self-employment, and new national qualifications frameworks. In general, Anglophone countries have gone farther along this reform route than their Francophone neighbors. At the 1998 Conference of Ministers of Education of Countries Sharing the French Language (CONFEMEN) conference in Bamako, Mali, Francophone education ministers adopted a very well-targeted program of policy reform, but implementation has been slow (Johanson and Adams 2004).

Some of the skills needed for growth and competitiveness can be anticipated. Others cannot be. The most promising approach for building appropriate skills in a setting where specific skill needs are unpredictable has four elements. The *first* is to concentrate on building the *generic* skills in secondary education that can provide the basis for further learning. The *second* is to provide more flexibility to graduates of vocational and technical programs by consolidating specializations into broader families of occupations with broader application prospects. The *third* is to make secondary and higher education programs demand driven, and to improve the information that parents and students use to choose among educational options. The *fourth* is to develop a range of opportunities for adult retraining and learning (World Bank 2008b).

Future development assistance. The following funding priorities have been proposed for development partners:

- public-private partnerships in which governments encourage non-governmental providers to collaborate with employers;
- development of demand-responsive national training systems that involve all stakeholders;
- decentralization of state-sponsored technical education;
- introduction of formula funding that rewards performance and outcomes; and
- development of associations of nongovernmental training providers, as well as trade and sector associations. The former is to advocate for their interests and deliver training relevant to their members (Johanson and Adams 2004).

Tertiary Education

Despite recent reform efforts, and significant achievements by some institutions, tertiary education systems in Sub-Saharan Africa have not yet adapted to the new rules of play imposed by a global knowledge economy. Let us assess their progress and shortcomings in eight determinant aspects of tertiary education performance: strategic orientation, autonomy and accountability, governance, management, financing, relevance, research and development, and regional collaboration. This will be done first at the level of tertiary education systems, where "systemic" policy approaches constitute a fairly recent way of thinking about education, and then at the level of tertiary institutions, which has been the more common analytical method.

Strategic orientation. The massification of enrollments has focused public concern on tertiary education, as its costs have forced governments and citizens alike to dig deeper into their purses. The knowledge intensity of economic competition has pushed this concern into the realm of strategic management. Countries begin to see their tertiary education subsector as a composite whole rather than as a collection of individual institutions. As systemic perspectives become common, tertiary institutes take on greater strategic importance as elements of a national innovation system. The innovation system perspective assumes that:

- the system is made up of complementary components, and thus the performance of the system depends as much on the strength of these components as it does on their interactive linkages;
- system performance also relies on coordinating mechanisms or bridging institutions that monitor, steer, and facilitate its inter-actions; and
- change occurs simultaneously from the top down and the bottom up, with the consequence that innovation and adaptation (and hence institutional learning) can occur at any point in the system (Bleiklie, Laredo, and Sorlin 2007).

Growing consideration of strategic orientation provides the basis for tertiary policy attention to institutional differentiation, quality assur-ance, system oversight bodies, competitive funding, externally account-able governance, and more businesslike management. As this orientation takes root, the goal of optimizing economic competitiveness replaces institutional egalitarianism as the basis for policy decision making (Bleiklie, Laredo, and Sorlin 2007).[11] With this, strategic management is increasingly applied to the tertiary education system, leading the prime minister of Malaysia to declare in 2006 that, "For most countries today, human resource development and human capital formation is either extremely important, absolutely vital, or a matter of life or death. In the case of Malaysia . . . we think it is a matter of life or death" (Association of Commonwealth Universities 2006).

As part of the effort to inject strategic orientation into the tertiary edu-cation system, SSA countries are now beginning to review national policies concerning the role of the private sector in the education system. These policies sometimes include overly restrictive or controlling regulations; cumbersome registration procedures that are less transparent than they should be; imposition of unclear and subjective criteria and standards to qualify for registration; outdated criteria for accreditation that emphasize the number of books available in hard copy and take no account of access to electronic materials; limits on the ability of private education institutions to set tuition fees at market rates; criteria relating to financial reserves, land area, and infrastructure owned by private institutions; lengthy curriculum and program approval processes (up to three or four years); and restrictions on political or religious aspects of curriculum content (Fielden and LaRocque 2008).

In the public sector, SSA countries are beginning to formulate national plans for tertiary education development and link them to their economic growth strategies. In different ways, Ethiopia, Kenya, Mozambique, Nigeria, South Africa, and Tanzania have recently sought to do this. At the institutional level, however, strategic plans tend to be shaped in response to autonomously defined mission statements, rather than linked to national economic and education development strategies, as has been practiced in Australia. This suggests the need for better correspondence between the strategic plans of tertiary institutions and the larger systemic strategies for tertiary education and overall national development.

From a strategic perspective, the messages of this study are essentially three. Where conditions justify, SSA countries could consider the development of at least one "flagship" tertiary institution with a capacity to teach and conduct research at something approaching an international standard so that the country possesses a capacity to link up with global knowledge resources. Within tertiary institutions, strategic focus on strengthening those disciplines deemed most relevant to a country's economy and future growth prospects is recommended. In addition, tertiary students should be competitively selected on the basis of academic merit, even though this may have equity or distributional consequences, in order to ensure an acceptable level of quality and potential among future graduates. The expectation here is that a small number of highly skilled and talented people will be able to catalyze a shift in industry toward activities that are technology intensive and add more value domestically.

At both the system and institutional levels, however, local political dynamics can undermine even the best strategic plans. For instance, Senegal put in place during the early 1990s a well-conceived and apparently consensus-based reform program for Cheikh Anta Diop University. But following national elections won by the opposition party, the reform program was overturned (Eisemon and Salmi 1993). Likewise, strong staff unions and student associations can stalemate tertiary reform efforts when they feel that their interests are threatened, e.g., Ghana, Mali, Nigeria, Senegal.

Autonomy and accountability. Autonomy for a tertiary institution commonly means that it exercises control over its student admissions, financial expenditures, and personnel decisions. In practice, wide variation in institutional autonomy can be found across nations. Yet trends of growing autonomy with increased expectations of accountability are evident worldwide (Bleiklie, Laredo, and Sorlin 2007). Under shifting market conditions, institutions argue for greater autonomy in order to possess the flexibility that enables the innovation, reform, and management initiative necessary to meet specific performance goals linked to accountability. For these reasons, greater management freedom has recently been awarded to tertiary institutions in Denmark, Germany, Indonesia, Japan, Sweden, and Thailand (Bladh 2007; Salmi 2007).[12] However, increased autonomy does not mean less external control, as governments, parliaments, and societal interest groups are asking for increased accountability (Fielden 2007). Thus, the field of contest often resides in institutional governance arrangements.

For the most part, African tertiary institutions are either run as part and parcel of the state apparatus (for example, in many of the Francophone countries), or are provided with a degree of independence in the form of their own governing body with statutory powers and responsibilities (more common in Anglophone countries).[13] But these distinctions may become blurred as governments of both regions have strived to ensure strong relations of political accountability between institutional leaders and the head of state. Thus, the details of who participates in institutional governance and management, and how these individuals are selected, have a direct bearing on the institution's capabilities for flexible response to changing circumstances and innovative initiatives to take advantage of emerging opportunities.

Accountability is a more recent construct, emerging from the 21st century mix of market ideology, democratization, and the increased competition for public resources. It calls for tertiary institutions to demonstrate the relevance of their activities to the needs of society, and to allow their effectiveness in performing this role to be assessed by external review (Ade, Goma, and Johnson 1996). To this end, institutional governance arrangements have been modified to incorporate greater stakeholder representation.[14] Other mechanisms of accountability include licensing requirements, academic audits, quality assurance reviews, accreditation, learning assessment tests, professional qualification exams, and performance-based budgeting. These mechanisms seek to monitor the extent of coverage (access), the fairness of coverage (equity), educational quality, relevance to the labor market and national needs, values imparted (citizenship), use of resources (efficiency), and the financial capacity of the institution to maintain standards (sustainability). It should be recognized that some accountability goals may be incompatible and stakeholder interests may conflict (Salmi 2007).

Accountability has also been consciously pursued within African tertiary education. Fifteen SSA countries now possess formal quality assurance mechanisms, up from just three in 1990 (Materu 2007).[15] Nigeria has introduced an attention-grabbing national ranking of universities and academic programs; Kenya is reportedly considering something similar. Although most tertiary institutions are required to submit to annual financial audits, relatively few are legally obligated to submit annual public reports covering outputs and achievements. In fact, a review of tertiary legislation in 20 African countries found that 15 of them make no mention of annual reporting requirements (Lao 2007).

In SSA countries, the tension between the demands for accountability and needs for autonomy often leads to a review of the legal frameworks applicable both to the tertiary system and to individual institutions. Since 2000, updates in national higher education acts have been undertaken in 10 countries, and six institutions have revised their university acts (Bloom, Canning, and Chan 2006a; Lao 2007).[16] The newer higher education laws in Africa tend to increase university autonomy at the upper levels of governance, while reducing it internally. Thus, the position of university chancellor has been progressively delinked from the office of the head of state (e.g. Ghana, Nigeria, South Africa, Tanzania), and government membership in institutional governing councils has been reduced or offset by an increase in private sector representatives (e.g., University of Mauritius, University of Zambia). At the same time, internal decision making based on collegial consensus is giving way to more "corporativist" approaches characterized by strategic planning, strengthened managerial structures, and some dilution of the power of academic committees. In light of the rapid growth of many institutions, it could hardly be otherwise.

Governance. Not long ago, when SSA tertiary education was often comprised of a few publicly financed institutions operating within less democratic political systems, university governance was frequently cast in terms of adversarial government-university relations (Ajayi, Goma, and Johnson 1996). Today, with enrollment growth, increased numbers of public and private institutions, the movement toward cost-sharing, and the growth of democracy, this relationship is becoming more of a partnership. Government officials increasingly view tertiary education as a competitive asset that should be carefully managed in the national interest. For their part, academic staff is gradually more accepting of university governance as a broader stakeholder organization in place of the former "republic of scholars" managed by the university community.

As tertiary institutions have grown in size, two levels of governance have emerged. One guides the overall fortunes of the institution (i.e., the governing board or council), and the other oversees the academic programs (i.e., the academic board or senate). Good institutional performance stems from an effective relationship between the policy making of the governance body and the policy implementation responsibilities of management.

The governing board must be large enough to incorporate the range of professional expertise needed to conduct its affairs, but small enough to function expeditiously.[17] Ideally, 60 percent of this group should come from outside the institution itself. Conscious efforts may be needed to ensure that the board includes skills in management, financial administration, human resources development, law, property management, and other areas relevant to challenges faced by the institution. For this reason, members are best selected by a nominating committee comprised of the institutional head and several members of the governing board itself, rather than via external appointment by the government.

The academic board is responsible for academic policy and quality standards. It is likely to function best with around three dozen members; more will make it unwieldy. Its standing committees should address academic topics such as curriculum, quality assurance, staff development, and information access, but not engage in issues of finance, institutional development, or procurement.

In the face of rapid changes, larger institutions may want to consider establishing a joint strategy committee that spans the governing and academic boards. Comprised of no more than a dozen persons, it should be led by the institution's chief executive and include the chair of the governing board, the chairs of the board's finance and physical development committees, the institution's most senior academic and administrative officers, and three or four deans elected by the academic board (Daniel 2007).

As student cost-sharing becomes more common, student representation in the institution's governance bodies at all levels is appropriate. A UNESCO survey of European countries found that 31 out of 36 have legal requirements for student representation, and the most common proportion of students in total board membership was between 10 percent and 20 percent (Daniel 2007). In SSA, student representation is also legally mandated on virtually all governing boards, but its share of board membership is commonly lower at 3 percent to 10 percent (Lao 2007).

Management. Driven by globalization, democratization, and tertiary massification, trends in autonomy and accountability impact not only tertiary governance, but tertiary management as well. At the tertiary system level, the rise of "system support bodies" can be observed. These can include steering or oversight agencies, quality assurance bodies, and student financial assistance programs. For example, since 2000, national councils or commissions of higher tertiary education have been established in Botswana, Ethiopia, Rwanda, Tanzania, and Uganda to oversee the development of their tertiary systems. Such semiautonomous "buffer" bodies are less common in Francophone Africa, where the norm has been instead to create separate ministries of higher education. One advantage of a buffer body is that it removes detailed operational issues from ministry of education responsibility. This protects the state from charges of intervention in academic affairs, encourages greater institutional autonomy, and saves the legislature from becoming the target for regular lobbying (Fielden 2007).

At the institutional level, many public African universities have now become large and complex organizations. No longer is it possible for an esteemed professor to oversee a few thousand students and a couple hundred staff on a face-to-face basis. This has prompted growing interest in "businesslike" approaches to management within public tertiary institutions. For example, a "management team" comprised of the institution's senior administrative officers is often established to set management priorities and coordinate associated actions on a weekly or biweekly basis.

Other new businesslike management functions are being adopted by tertiary institutions worldwide. Among them are strategic planning, market research, research management, financial development planning, and performance management (Salmi 2007; Bleiklie, Laredo, and Sorlin 2007). This places a growing premium on leadership and management capacities within tertiary institutions, triggering regional efforts by the Association of African Universities and the Southern African Regional Universities Association to professionalize these skills, and make a more conscious effort to develop management skills within institutions. In addition, growing interest in the establishment of formal training programs in higher education management can be observed within Kenya, Nigeria, and South Africa.

One frequently underdeveloped area of management in larger institutions is human resource or personnel management. Staffing issues of all types are frequently handled by academic staff, such as faculty deans or departmental heads, whose main responsibilities are not in administration. They may devote as much as half their time to personnel management matters, even though they are likely to have received little or no training in human resource administration. This is inefficient for supervisors and may contribute to staff disgruntlement. For example, slow decision making and lack of transparency in personnel matters were found to be a factor contributing to brain drain in a survey of African universities (Tettey 2006). More important, tertiary staff with postgraduate degrees increasingly operate within the expanding global labor market for skilled human resources and aspire to levels of remuneration broadly comparable with those of their peers overseas. Thus, credentialed academicians confront real opportunity costs every day that they spend living in a low-wage economy. To reduce the burden of this sacrifice, university staff often seek to minimize the time spent on their institutional responsibilities in order to maximize the time available for other income-generating activities. Thus, given their inability to raise salaries, institutional managers face great difficulties in recruiting, motivating, and retaining staff.[18]

Another challenge to personnel management is the permanence of institutional staffing profiles and the consequent inability of institutions to adjust to change—either in labor market demands for skills, the emergence of new academic disciplines, or the rapidly evolving frontiers of scientific knowledge—through strategic adjustments in staffing. In most tertiary institutions, especially universities, staff appointments are likely to be linked to civil service regulations, and tenure may be awarded within a few years of initial hire. This creates a paradox in which many institutions are left to face tomorrow's challenges with yesterday's staffing configurations. A bold attempt to overturn this longstanding constraint is currently under way in Uganda, where a government white paper abolishing tenure is being prepared for cabinet approval. Instead, academic staff would be hired on short-term contracts of three to five years duration, renewable based on good performance (Butagira and Nandutu 2008). Pakistan is in the process of doing likewise.

African tertiary institutions may therefore find it useful to set up a small professional office of human resource development in order to standardize and monitor personnel decisions, and to train academic supervisors in the best practices of personnel management. These could include: the development of job descriptions for employees; development of a staffing profile for the institution as a framework for appointments and promotions; establishment of orientation programs for newly appointed staff; setting up a staff performance management system with clear evaluation criteria and a standard reward structure; creating a common system for staff leave; and determining training and professional development needs of staff (Daniel 2007).

Financing. Financing is the foremost hurdle confronting the managers of SSA's tertiary education sector. As tertiary institutions have become more numerous and enrollments have soared, the financing of tertiary education has become more complex and challenging—and the source of considerable political contention (Woodhall 2007). In various countries, public funding of public tertiary institutions has declined in importance as government revenues are stretched to meet competing needs. Not only has this created space for the emergence of private providers, but public institutions have been pushed to develop capacities for income generation and to use their resources frugally. Figure 3.1 depicts four different paths in this journey. In East Africa, the successful introduction of cost-sharing has enabled countries to reduce the share of tertiary expenditures within their education budgets even as enrollments increased. In Southern Africa, a more cautious approach to both enrollment growth

Figure 3.1   Tertiary Share of Education Budget by Region, 1975–2005

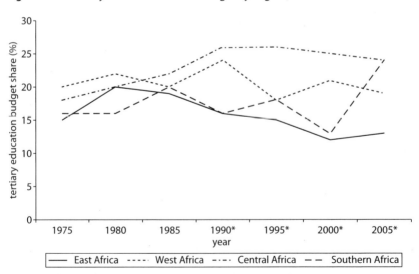

Sources: UNESCO; EdStats; World Bank 1988, * or closest available year; *Higher Education in Developing Countries: Peril and Promise*, 2000; World Bank data; Brossard and Foko, 2007.

and cost-sharing worked well until 2000, when the explosion of enroll-ments without commensurate gains in cost-sharing triggered a sharp rise in the tertiary share of the education budget. In West Africa, gradual reductions in student welfare allowances have helped to rein in tertiary budget shares since their peak in 1990. But in Central Africa, an inability to manage costs as enrollments have risen has generated a sustained high level of tertiary expenditure within education budgets. Notably, Brossard and Foko (2007) find that student welfare expenses still comprise a ques-tionably high average of 45 percent of tertiary education budgets in SSA Francophone countries. These resources could be better used to shore up educational quality and relevance.

In response to financing challenges, institutions worldwide are devel-oping stakeholder support networks, fostering alumni organizations, establishing business partnerships, and giving heightened attention to the elimination of inefficiencies.[19] The latter brings greater management attention to staff-student ratios, to student repetition and drop-out rates, and to outsourcing nonacademic services such as security, maintenance, and groundskeeping. As quality-based competition intensifies, tertiary insti-tutions are beginning to venture into the difficult, but potentially ben-eficial, field of performance incentive schemes for raising output in teaching, research, and income generation.

Within Africa, many of these same trends can be observed.[20] For exam-ple, inefficient staff/student ratios pointed out two decades ago (World Bank 1988) have largely disappeared as the result of surging enrollments combined with staff recruitment and retention difficulties (see table 3.4). In fact, overcrowding has frequently replaced underutilization as a major management challenge on many campuses. The outsourcing of nonacad-emic services has become increasingly common, enabling institutions to concentrate their resources on the teaching and learning process. Recent progress in income generation and diversification has enabled institutions to venture beyond financial survivalism, to reduce funding dependence

Table 3.4   Average Staff/Student Ratios for SSA Universities

Region	1990	2002
Sub-Saharan Africa	14/7	20/6
East Africa	9/1	20/3
West Africa	14/2	26/7
Central Africa	12/8	17/5
Southern Africa	8/7	11/2

Sources: EdStats; Saint 1992.

on government, and to provide managers with occasional resources for experimentation and innovation.

Only performance incentive schemes remain as largely uncharted territory on the African continent. At the system level, interest in funding allocation formulae is appearing as a means of simultaneously encouraging performance and efficiency. South Africa adopted a formula-based funding system in 2001, combining block grants based on teaching inputs, graduate outputs, and research productivity with earmarked funds for redress and development. Nigeria is in the process of aligning its funding with the "carrying capacity" of institutions. Ethiopia is developing a formula that takes into account the discipline composition, gender balance, and research productivity of each institution. Ghana, Kenya, and Mozambique are considering similar formula-based approaches.

As governments have moved toward increased cost-sharing by students and parents, additional resources have been drawn into beleaguered tertiary education systems. In Africa, this has often taken the form of "parallel" programs, "self-sponsored" students, or facilities "user fees" (Court 1999; Ishengoma 2004; Kiamba 2004; Johnstone 2006). Ethiopia has introduced a form of graduate tax (Tekleselassie 2002; Yizengaw 2006). Funds generated by these innovations have been used to improve staff salaries, strengthen retirement pensions, upgrade teaching facilities, and improve libraries. But cost-sharing has also underscored the need for student financial support in the form of loans and grants (Johnstone 2004). In response, student financial assistance schemes have recently been inaugurated in Namibia, Rwanda, Tanzania, and Uganda. These initiatives have often been informed by prior experience with, and the lessons learned from, recent reforms to more established student loan programs in Ghana (ICHEFAP 2007), Kenya (Otieno 2004), and South Africa (Van Harte 2002), which have wrestled with challenges of students defaulting on their loans, high administrative costs, and difficulty assessing student need. Lessons learned from Latin American student loan programs have also been helpful (Salmi 1999).

At the level of institutions, financial administration continues to be an important target for capacity-building efforts. Very few SSA tertiary institutions have yet invested the effort to prepare medium- and long-term financial development plans. In numerous cases, weak accounting and reporting systems make budget monitoring difficult. When this occurs, the financial position of the institution is often poorly understood, and this compromises good decision making. Perhaps to compensate for such weaknesses, some institutions suffer from an excess of internal controls, which slow administrative processes and unnecessarily consume the time of managers. For example, delegation of expenditure authority may be limited, forcing senior officers to approve relatively minor and routine payments. The finance office often communicates poorly and infrequently with teaching departments and other organizational units, adding to the difficulty of identifying and addressing financial problems. Although an increasing number of tertiary institutions have computerized their financial accounts and made efforts to strengthen their financial administration, financial monitoring reports have not yet gained widespread acceptance as a basic management tool.

At this point, the future financial challenges for most SSA tertiary education systems will be how to obtain more public funds, how to leverage greater funding from nonpublic sources, and how to use available funds more efficiently (Mingat, Ledoux, and Rakotomalala 2008). SSA currently invests 4.5 percent of GDP in education, up from 4.0 percent in 1988, and this is high by international standards (see table 3.5). As a result, many African nations are approaching the limits of the share of public resources that can reasonably be expected for use in education development. Similarly, many countries are at or above the 20 percent ceiling that is generally appropriate for tertiary education's share of the education budget (World Bank 2002). In light of Education for All gains in access to basic education, and the growing pressures that these will generate for secondary education in the years ahead, it is not realistic to think that tertiary education might receive more than a temporary boost beyond this ceiling. Likewise, tertiary institutions have generally approached the limits of what is possible in terms of income generation, and significant breakthroughs in this area are unlikely. Last, students and families—whether through tuition fees, parallel programs, earmarked charges, or the acceptance of loan obligations—are often contributing their share, although scope for further private contribution generally remains in Francophone countries, as well as in tertiary systems where the lion's share of students come from the richest

Table 3.5   Public Expenditure on Education as a Percentage of GDP, 2004

Region/World	Percentage
Middle East and North Africa	4.9
Sub-Saharan Africa	4.5
Latin America and Caribbean	4.4
South and West Asia	3.6
East Asia and Pacific	2.8
World	4.3

Source: UNESCO Global Education Digest 2007.

households. In short, government, institutions, and individuals in a signifi-cant number of SSA countries are currently doing nearly as much as they can in financing tertiary education, and this is why the focus must now turn to the task of fund-raising from nontraditional sources and using existing resources more efficiently.

Increasing efficiency levels in resource use will require political will, pol-icy consensus, and management acumen, as inevitably the solutions will mean setting aside the tradition of equitable sharing of funding across insti-tutions and programs in favor of hard choices concerning strategic priorities, comparative advantages, incentive systems, and calculated innovations. For example, governments could encourage private tertiary education to expand in the low-cost areas of business studies, social sciences, languages, and humanities so that public funds might progressively be withdrawn from these areas and concentrated on the strengthening of more expensive disciplines, such as sciences, engineering, and medicine.

Increasing efficiency also means tackling the elite privilege provided by large scholarship funds for students, some of which are managed directly by the office of the president rather than the ministry of education. In Lesotho, for example, tertiary bursaries consume 57 percent of the recur-rent tertiary budget (World Bank 2005). In 10 Francophone countries, scholarships for overseas study represent an average 14 percent of the ter-tiary education budget (Brossard and Foko 2007). A more efficient approach would restrict government sponsorship of students to only those discipline areas deemed most critical for the country's future devel-opment, consequently obliging those wishing to study in other areas to finance this from nonpublic sources.

Whereas the costs of providing primary and secondary education are determined largely by cost structures in local currency surrounding salaries, building materials, printing, and transportation, the cost structure for tertiary education, and especially university education, contains a large element of international expenditures in foreign exchange. It is hard to imagine a university without textbooks, reference books, academic jour-nals, laboratory equipment, technical instrumentation, computers, and instructional materials. In most African countries, all or most of these edu-cational inputs must be imported. Other regular expenses also reflect the inherently international nature of higher education: telecommunications, staff travel, international postage, spare parts, and overseas staff develop-ment. Primary or secondary teachers are unlikely to attend an international conference, but tertiary instructors, especially if they are engaged in research, see peer interaction at the regional and global levels as a normal aspect of their job descriptions as academics. More important, staff employed in primary and secondary education find that career advancement opportunities are determined largely by the local job market, but tertiary staff with postgraduate degrees, especially a PhD, increasingly operate within the expanding global labor market for skilled human resources, and aspire to levels of remuneration broadly comparable with those of their peers overseas. For these reasons, the comparative advantage of donor funding would seem to lie in the provision of hard currencies to address the foreign exchange needs of the education system. As suggested above, these needs are likely to be the greatest at the higher levels of education.

Relevance. Global competitiveness puts a premium on the relevance of education to the needs of the country and its employers. In the past, educational quality and relevance were often viewed as synonymous; high-quality education was relevant education. But no longer. Today it is possible to have high-quality education that is irrelevant to a country's ambitions, or to the regional economy surrounding a university campus. Irrelevant education increases the chances of graduate unemployment and brain drain, and deprives a nation of an important instrument for its development.

At the level of tertiary education systems, relevance is embedded in the profile of core competencies possessed by the aggregate of tertiary graduates. African countries have long used the guideline of a 60:40 division between sciences/engineering and arts/humanities, agreed to in 1962 at a UNESCO/UNECA regional higher education conference in Antananarivo, Madagascar, as a reference for graduate output. But this guideline has no empirical justification (World Bank 2006; Daniel 2007). Among the countries in the world with higher S&T shares of total tertiary enrollments (30 percent to 35 percent) are Ireland, Korea, Japan, and Sweden—but also Ghana, Kenya, Mozambique, and South Africa.[21] Lacking clear guidelines, it is advisable that tertiary institutions incorporate core competencies necessary for understanding science, technology, business, and society into a set of universitywide required courses for all students. Such a "skills and knowledge" approach empowers graduates to be effective contributors to the economy and society. In Ghana, the privately run Ashesi University College is quietly but creatively employing this approach to offer relevant African tertiary education for the twenty-first century.

Similar experimentation and adaptation of the traditional university mission are generating pertinent models of tertiary education elsewhere on the continent. Today the notion of the African "development university"

(Yesufu 1973) is being redefined. Whereas the original label referred to a partnership between the nascent national university and the national government in a joint quest for national development, the "development university" of today is more likely to be characterized in the context of its regional economy or geographical catchment area. Jimma University in Ethiopia has pioneered community-based education in the country, through which it requires tertiary students in medicine, agriculture, and other professions to engage local communities, to learn from them, and to pursue problem solving with them. A kindred approach guides the University for Development Studies in northern Ghana. In Senegal, the Université Gaston Berger Saint-Louis du Sénégal seeks to develop applied expertise on the Sahel region. In Rwanda, the Kigali Institute of Science and Technology promotes low-cost technological solutions to local problems of energy supply, waste management, and postharvest processing. In Kenya, a new university structured around a multidisciplinary approach to development in semiarid areas has been proposed. In these ways, African tertiary institutions are seeking to differentiate themselves from one another in the quest for relevance, as well as from the traditional models rooted in the colonial experience.

Striving for relevance through a differentiated yet articulated array of tertiary institutions has been more common elsewhere in the world than in Africa. Differentiation is a process of increasing institutional specialization with the goal of improving the effectiveness of the overall system. It occurs as follows. For tertiary institutions to become more responsive to the needs of the knowledge society, they must give conscious attention to the "fitness for purpose" of their outputs. The way to do this is by developing specialized missions and institutional profiles, and the end result of this process is a differentiated tertiary education system. The differentiation profile for tertiary education in several selected African countries is provided in table 3.6.

The case for differentiation rests on several arguments. First, a diversified system improves access for students with different educational backgrounds and abilities by providing a wider range of choices and diverse pedagogical orientations. Second, it facilitates social mobility by offering multiple entry points to tertiary education and various options for successful students to transfer on to higher levels of study. Third, it responds to labor market needs by providing the growing range of specializations needed for economic and social development. Fourth, differentiation provides interest groups with opportunities to strengthen their sense of identity and political legitimization by enabling them to target

Table 3.6   Differentiation Profiles for Selected African Tertiary Systems

Country	Public univ.	Private univ.	Public polytechnic or prof. inst.	Private polytechnic or prof. inst.	Public technical colleges	Private technical colleges
Cameroon	6	20	3	X	X	X
Ghana	7	28	10	0	n.t.	n.t.
Kenya	7	17	4	0	n.t.	n.t.
Malawi	2	2	2	1	X	X
Mozam-bique	3	5	8	6	n.t.	n.t.
Nigeria	50	25	51	6	46	9
Rwanda	2	6	4	4	4	4
Senegal	2	3	15	44	X·	X
South Africa	22	3	0	0	100	350
Tanzania	8	13	15	X	X	X
Uganda	4	13	1	X	67	X
Zambia	2	5	0	0	3	n.t.

Source: Ng'ethe et al. 2007.
Note: X = in existence, but data not available.
n.t. = not included in tertiary system.

specific student populations (e.g., women, regional cultures, religious communities). Fifth, it increases the effectiveness of institutions by encouraging them to specialize in what they do best. Finally, it permits low-risk experimentation, whereby institutions can assess the viability of innovations created by others without having to adopt them directly (Van Vught 2007).

Whether differentiation practice conforms to this theory is less clear. Studies of American and European tertiary systems have concluded that differentiation is not necessarily associated with capacity development (Birnbaum 1983; Rhoades 1990; Huisman, Meek, and Wood 2007). Most often, tertiary systems have used any additional resources to replicate existing institutional models rather than to diversify institutional missions and modes of delivery. Some observers have also argued that accreditation requirements create a push for standardization that undermines diversity (Fried, Glass, and Baumgartl 2007).

In Africa, the differentiation picture is equally clouded. Differentiation has been enhanced by the recent explosion of private tertiary education, the establishment of specialized institutions focusing on distance learning, the education of women, or science and technology, and the efforts of some institutional mission statements to address community needs.

But it has been undercut by the upgrading of colleges and polytechnics to university status without filling the niches they leave behind, by required tutorial relationships in which established institutions shape the aspirations and work environments of new institutions, and by social demands that press for replication of the most prestigious institutional models (Ng'ethe, Subotzky, and Afeti 2007). In this regard, the lack of public attention to strengthening and updating the continent's polytechnics is particularly worrisome in light of their potential to contribute skilled problem solvers to the economy.

As SSA tertiary systems become larger and more diverse, governments are giving growing policy attention to the benefits of system articulation. Articulation refers to the procedures and mechanisms—the "bridges and ladders"—that permit student mobility, either across academic programs within a single institution or among different types of tertiary institutions within the same system. Although somewhat demanding in terms of its requirements for data collection, recordkeeping, and information management, articulation can do much to improve overall system efficiency. It does this by enabling students to have "second chances" if their education is unavoidably interrupted or if they discover they have made an incorrect career choice.

Articulation is normally operationalized through an academic credit accumulation and transfer system. South Africa has put such a system in place with its National Qualifications Framework. Cameroon, Malawi, and Rwanda have done likewise, and Mozambique expects to follow in the course of 2008. Among the Francophone countries, a movement to standardize academic degrees into an LMD (*licence, masters, doctorate*) structure, prompted by a similar effort within the European Union ("the Bologna Process"), is laying the foundation for greater student mobility and recognition of degree equivalence. Likewise, the Southern African Regional Universities Association (SARUA) and the Inter-University Council for East Africa (IUCEA) are taking steps to promote improved system articulation and student mobility among their member countries. At the continent level, the African Union, Association of African Universities, and UNESCO are working to obtain governments' ratification of an African Quality Rating Mechanism and strategy for harmonization, which would progressively move national tertiary education systems toward common regional standards of quality.

At the institutional level, the challenges of relevance assume multiple forms. Tertiary institutions are increasingly asked to be market oriented and demand responsive. They are pushed to identify labor market demands through employer surveys and graduate tracer studies. They are encouraged to ascertain student demands through market research. At the same time, they are urged to update their curricula to keep abreast of world knowledge, and to reform pedagogical methods to impart the soft skills deemed necessary to be productive in today's world. Moreover, rising emphasis on performance benchmarking in terms of national or international standards seeks to define relevance in terms of performance indicators.

Research and development. Knowledge generated and adapted through tertiary-level R&D activities—whether in graduate programs, academic research, or publicly supported research institutes—is the second leg (in addition to skilled workers) of the knowledge economy. African nations have sought to preserve and boost their capacities for R&D since 1964, when they pledged to devote 0.5 percent of their GDP to scientific research. Recognizing the growing importance of knowledge-generation capacities for economic competitiveness, they increased this commitment to 1 percent of GDP in 1980 (OAU 1990). However, achievement has fallen far short of this target. For example, Botswana, Burkina Faso, Namibia, Tanzania, Zambia, and Zimbabwe all spend less than 0.5 percent of GDP on research and development (Mouton 2008).

Tertiary institutions hold the potential to be major contributors to national knowledge generation. To tap this potential, governments across the globe have been setting national research priorities, crafting supportive policies, and creating new institutions to fund and otherwise support research capacity expansion efforts. This course has also been pursued by some African nations. For instance, Mozambique has issued a cabinet-approved national science, technology and innovation policy, and coupled this with a national research fund directed toward government research priorities. Nigeria has established a national science foundation to play a similar role, and Kenya is likely to do the same. At the same time, the capacity of the African Academy of Sciences to contribute professionally to such undertakings is being upgraded through a partnership with the National Academy of Sciences in the United States financed by the Bill & Melinda Gates Foundation.

Many African countries support publicly financed research institutes that could become building blocks in a national innovation system. But fairly daunting obstacles currently stand in the way of such aspirations. Reviewing national research institutes in 17 SSA countries, Mouton (2008) found many of them to be fragile, underresourced, vulnerable to the vagaries of political events, and buffeted by frequent government shifts in ministerial responsibility for science and technology. He concludes that they are trapped in a "subsistence mode" in which they produce knowledge largely for their own use, contributing little to their societies and the world beyond.

Within individual SSA tertiary institutions, research has often fallen victim to the increased teaching workload generated by enrollment expansion and the need for staff to supplement inadequate academic salaries with consultancies or nonacademic work. This decline in research output has often been paralleled by the widespread reductions in public funding for research. In the process, graduate students comprise a shrinking portion of total enrollments, reducing the next generation of tertiary instructors and researchers at a time when their numbers should ideally be increasing.[22]

To their credit, tertiary institutions have sought ways to improve their terms and conditions of service so that capable staff might be recruited and retained within the constraining parameters of public service pay scales. For example, several countries have introduced salary top-ups for this purpose. However, in an era when brain power contributes significantly to competitive advantage among nations and graduate degree holders are increasingly mobile, ad hoc solutions are unlikely to be more than stopgap measures. At some point, serious consideration will need to be given to attracting (including from abroad) and retaining productive academics and researchers through an explicit two-tier salary system in which staff can expect to see superior performances rewarded with tenure and a significant improvement in remuneration.[23] Without such measures, it will be difficult for African tertiary institutions to lay the foundations for research universities that may progressively aspire to world-ranking status.

One promising approach to boosting the relevance of teaching and research programs among tertiary institutions is the use of competitively accessed innovation funds. An innovation fund is a pool of discretionary funds that is earmarked for one or more uses. Funds are normally accessed on a phased or competitive basis using a transparent process of proposal submission, peer review, and management approval. The distribution of funds is usually implemented through performance agreements that include previously defined measurable outcome indicators. In tertiary education, innovation funds have been used to improve the quality of teaching, research, and community service activities, as well as to strengthen university linkages with regional and national development efforts. They have also been used to build management capacities, stimulate research, encourage cross-discipline or inter-institutional collaboration, and focus institutional attention on new or emerging issues of policy importance (Saint 2006). Within Africa, they have been used in Ethiopia (Development Innovation Fund), Ghana (Teaching and Learning Innovation Fund), Mozambique (Quality Improvement Fund), South Africa (Technology and Human Resources for Industry Programme), and Tanzania (Commission for Science and Technology).

Regional collaboration. Regional and subregional networks frequently provide the means for national tertiary systems and institutions to "bridge" into the sphere of experiences, best practices, and innovation that exist at the international level, and to use scarce resources more efficiently. This was recognized early on at the 1985 ECA/African Association of Universities (AAU) conference in Mbabane, Swaziland, which issued a call to action for multicountry collaboration in higher education (Economic Commission for Africa 1985). But at the end of the twentieth century, this middle ground between the local and the global was either barren or thinly populated in Africa. Exceptions existed, most notably the Association of African Universities, the Agence Universitaire de la Francophonie, and the African Network of Scientific and Technical Institutions. Yet for the most part, the mechanisms for cross-national communication, diffusion of innovation, exchange of lessons learned, orchestration of common interests, and sharing of resources had not yet appeared on the scene.

The germination of numerous mechanisms for subregional and regional collaboration in tertiary education is one of the visible characteristics of the current decade. At the continent level, the revamped African Union has chosen the revitalization of African tertiary education as one of its priority areas for its Second Decade of Education for Africa (2006–15) plan of action. Its associated New Partnership for Africa's Development has issued an action agenda for tertiary education focusing on funding, governance and management, quality assurance, and public-private partnerships. The Association of African Universities has teamed with the World Bank to build regionwide expertise in quality assurance, and with the U.K. Department for International Development to enhance the capacity of African higher education institutions and networks to support development. The Global Business School Network for Africa seeks to enhance the performance of business schools and improve the management talents of their graduates. To a large extent, this trend of increased cooperation has been facilitated by the parallel maturation of regional economic organizations such as SADC, Preferential Trade Area (PTA), and ECOWAS, and the associated growth of intercountry relationships; by the lower costs and increased ease of international communications associated with the Internet; and by the multiplication in the number of universities that enable broader load sharing.

Often the best route for establishing a regional center of excellence may be through the development of a strong national institution that progressively creates a regional sphere of attraction as its reputation grows. This has been the well-established role of Cheikh Anta Diop University in Dakar, Senegal, and more recently of the University of Cape Town in South Africa. This approach can also be applied to private institutions, as exemplified by Africa University, a private university in Zimbabwe that has been serving students from more than a half-dozen countries since 1992.

At the subregional level, revitalized older organizations are being joined by new ones in the task of tertiary education community building. In East Africa, the longstanding Inter-University Council for East Africa has introduced new quality guidelines for higher education regulators in Kenya, Tanzania, and Uganda in the effort to foster common regional standards of quality in higher learning. Its efforts are complemented by the Regional Universities Forum (RUFORUM), a consortium of 12 universities from seven countries that are working together to create and sustain regional postgraduate programs in agricultural disciplines. In West Africa, the venerable Conseil Africain et Malgache pour l'Enseignement Supérieur (CAMES) serves as a regional coordination agency for university activities in 17 Francophone countries, particularly with regard to quality assurance, research dissemination, and staff mobility. The more recent Council of Francophone University Rectors from Africa and the Indian Ocean (CRUFAOCI) seeks to strengthen ICT infrastructure and encourage regional doctoral programs. In Ouagadougou, the International Institute for Water and Environmental Engineering is a unique cooperative effort among the government of Burkina Faso, other African countries, and several international partners, which is building upon its strong record of postsecondary technologist training to expand its regional reach and launch postgraduate programs. In Southern Africa, the Southern African Regional Universities Association has put forward an ambitious subregional agenda of collaborative efforts targeting leadership development, ICT infrastructure expansion, science and technology promotion, and HIV/AIDS mitigation.

As early as 1980, the call went out across Africa for cross-country collaboration in postgraduate training (OAU 1990). Although the justification was clear—greater efficiency of resource use through economies of scale in the training of highly skilled specialists for smaller nations, or for important professions with limited local demand—the call at first went largely unanswered. A notable exception was the African Network of Scientific and Technical Institutions founded in 1980 to promote the pooling of resources within the region in the quest for higher quality training and research.[24] The idea of collaborative regional postgraduate training gained impetus in 1988 with the sustained success of the African Economic Research Consortium, initially at the master's level and since 2002, also at the PhD level (Lyakurwa 2004; World Bank 1991a). Gradually others followed suit. Today, some 23 regional master's programs and 10 regional PhD programs are operational (see Annex C). Appropriately, many of these address skill needs in agriculture, which is Africa's principal economic activity. Whereas all of these regional programs are based on cooperation among existing tertiary institutions, plans are advancing to construct regional campuses for several African Institutes of Science and Technology, initially in Nigeria, subsequently in Tanzania, and then in Southern Africa.

A possible model for a regional training approach to building capacities in the sciences may be the African Institute for Mathematical Sciences (AIMS). This is a regional postgraduate center in Cape Town, South Africa, that seeks to promote mathematics and science in Africa; to recruit and train talented students and teachers; and to build capacity for African initiatives in education, research, and technology. The institute is structured around a nine-month postgraduate course taught by outstanding African and international lecturers. The course develops strong mathematical and computing problem-solving skills, and leads to a postgraduate diploma in mathematical sciences. It is taught in association with the Faculty of Mathematics at the University of Cambridge, the Division of Mathematical, Physical and Life Sciences Division at the University of Oxford, and the University of Paris-Sud 11. The AIMS course is innovative in style and content. Lecturers engage with students and interact with them at all hours, during and outside of lectures. Lectures are often halted for discussion or to work in small groups. Problem-solving sessions are held each day so that material covered in the lectures is quickly assimilated and put into practice. Since opening in September 2003, AIMS has graduated 110 students (27 women) from three dozen countries.[25]

Accumulating experience with regional training programs suggests that they make sense where fixed costs are high and demand is clear but insufficient to reach a critical mass in each country, e.g., narrowly specialized technical fields, emerging new cross-disciplinary areas, small nations. Regional programs promise economies in assembling a critical mass of specialists. One hub location can serve the graduate training needs of a larger regional watershed; e.g. the highly effective University Science, Humanities and Engineering Partnerships in Africa (USHEPiA) program at the University of Cape Town. Minimum conditions for regional undertakings are: common problems and needs across regions; demonstrable economies of scale; an insufficient national training base, i.e. absence of duplication; staff/management buy-in at the host institution that may have other national priorities; and availability of financing to allow participation by students from nonhost countries. Above all, sustained financing commitments are the key to success. Adequate start-up support is required for designing, launching, and fine-tuning of the operations. Experience suggests that successful regional training programs will need long-term donor commitment, which best takes the form of consortia of multiple donors with complementary interests.

The risks and challenges of regional training programs have to be kept in mind. Building another layer of educational institutions can be risky, divisive, and expensive. Ideally, regional centers of excellence should evolve from existing strong national institutions, and not be created anew (InterAcademy Council 2004). Civil unrest in Côte d'Ivoire and Zimbabwe highlight the political risks of locating capacity-building programs in some countries. Failure of the regional MSc program in agricultural economics at the University of Nairobi as a result of withdrawal of donor funding is also instructive (InterAcademy Council 2004). Even through donors may underwrite a regional training program for a decade or longer, national political leaders have been reluctant to continue the program when development assistance comes to an end (Eicher 2006). This suggests that local ownership needs to be nurtured from the planning stage onward.

Regional collaboration in research possesses a slightly longer history. Various regional research networks were established during tertiary education's lean years of the 1980s and 1990s as a means of keeping some of the continent's best researchers engaged in scientific investigation. Notable among them have been the African Network of Scientific and Technical Institutions, the African Economic Research Consortium (AERC), and the Council for the Development of Social Science Research in Africa (CODESRIA). As the importance of knowledge partnerships is affirmed, the working relationships cultivated through these networks are now being applied to broader institutional linkage initiatives. For example, ANSTI has undertaken capacity assessments of staff, laboratories, and research equipment among science and engineering disciplines, and called for increased university-industry collaboration (ANSTI 2005a).

Cooperative approaches to regional research, when combined with strong international partnerships, can prove to be a powerful mechanism for addressing the challenges of African development. A superb example is the Malaria Research and Training Center established in 1992 by the government of Mali and developed in partnership with the U.S. National Institutes of Health, the World Health Organization, the University of Marseille (France), and La Sapienza University (Italy). Today it is a well-equipped research center that has trained numerous malaria researchers from neighboring countries, while making important scientific contributions to the monitoring and control of malaria. For example, the center discovered the malaria gene that provides resistance to chloroquine and developed molecular tools for standardizing the monitoring of malaria incidence within the region. Its applied research has also contributed to a fundamental change in the preventative treatment of malaria among pregnant women (MRTC 2005; World Bank Institute 2007)

Yet despite numerous tertiary education reform efforts in Sub-Saharan Africa, some of which are recognized above, the aggregate impact of these changes is not enough to develop the potential of tertiary institutions to become more significant contributors to economic and social development within their respective countries and within the region as a whole. For that to be achieved, tertiary institutions will need to consciously and persistently transform themselves into a different type of educational enterprise: networked, differentiated, and responsive institutions focused on the production of strategically needed human skills and applied problem-solving research. If achieved, this would constitute a twenty-first century version of the African "development university." What might be the process whereby such re-creation and renewal are achieved?

Concluding Observations: Tertiary Education for Competitiveness and Growth

The era of institutional individualism is rapidly passing. Today tertiary institutions are increasingly asked by their governments and their stakeholders to become team players—to contribute to a national innovation system that nourishes a national economic strategy (World Bank 2002; Agarwal 2006; Mashelkar 2007; Gore 2007; Lundvall 2007; Sonu 2007; Trinidade 2007). To play this role, they will need to put their legal autonomy into practice, become more entrepreneurial, embrace experimentation and change, see themselves as networked partners and institutional collaborators, understand the dynamic needs of the labor market, and strive for greater effectiveness in their approaches to teaching and research (World Bank 2002; World Bank Institute 2007). Although many may be reluctant to admit it, tertiary institutions are now becoming strategic national assets that can be steered and enabled by government policy to advance the national interest within the competitive dynamics of globalization. In short, a competitive economy now depends in part on a competitive tertiary education system.

Collectively, tertiary education systems in Africa have matured considerably over the past two decades. Yet individually they remain extraordinarily diverse. They range in size from 1,500 students in the Gambia to 1.4 million students in Nigeria. Access to tertiary education varies from 39 per 100,000 people in Malawi, to 1,500 per 100,000 people in South Africa. Public expenditure per tertiary student is US$7,742 in Lesotho, but only US$455 in Togo (see Annex D). Private provision accounts for 31 percent of tertiary enrollments in Côte d'Ivoire and Kenya, but only 1 percent in Mauritania. Some countries possess established postgraduate programs; others do not. Some have introduced specialized system support agencies such as national councils of tertiary education, quality assurance agencies, and student loan programs. ICT infrastructure and Internet connectivity are more pervasive in some countries than in others. And, of course, their economies are as diverse as their tertiary education systems.

Confronted by this wide array of circumstances (and varying degrees of political space for reform initiatives), general speculation regarding appropriate common tertiary education strategies for the region quickly loses value in the details of application. As a result, it is now far more appropriate for governments, together with their stakeholders and development partners, to seek country-specific solutions to the challenges of linking human resource development strategies with economic growth strategies. The arguments, examples, and lessons provided in this study, along with its annexes, are intended to stimulate dialogue to this end between those within the education sector and those outside of it. Because these two groups inevitably pursue differing interests, this dialogue will not be without tension. But those countries that can see the process through to a fruitful conclusion will be economically and socially healthier in the long run.

As Sub-Saharan countries seek to generate comparative economic advantages grounded in human resource development strategies, each country will have to map its own course, using its national development strategy and the lessons of good practice from other countries as navigational markers along the way (World Bank 2002). To assist with such undertakings, the following six generalized good practices—linked to issues raised earlier—may help to speed the journey toward a more effective and responsive tertiary education system.

- *Develop a strategy for national human resource development.*

As tertiary education becomes an important driver of economic growth, its most costly disciplines, sciences and engineering, are being targeted for particular emphasis in the midst of continued pressures for enrollment increases. Governments with little financial elbow room may have no alternative but to choose a limited number of priorities and fund them strategically at the expense of areas and activities that are ultimately considered to be of lesser importance (World Bank 2002). This option remains relatively untested in Africa, although it has proven successful in countries such as Brazil, Chile, and Korea. In those countries, the less expensive social sciences and humanities disciplines have increasingly been left to private provision, and governments have gradually concentrated their public investments in the development of science, engineering, and technology disciplines.[26]

The strategic approach selects certain discipline areas in which competent human resource development is judged to be vital for the success of economic development efforts in the country. For example, in the 1980s, Korea chose shipbuilding, electrical engineering, automotive engineering, management, and several other fields as critical human resource development areas in which to concentrate its education and training efforts. Ireland focused on pharmaceuticals and information technology. Singapore selected sciences and technologies linked to high-value medical equipment and services. Brazil developed expertise in aeronautical engineering, which launched its aircraft industry. In these cases, the goal is to produce graduates at an international standard in the chosen fields so that the country can become internationally competitive in terms of technical knowledge and competencies in a few strategically selected economic activities that hold a potential for good returns. The process of developing this strategy must go beyond the tertiary sector to involve government economic policy makers (who define the economic goals), and private sector representatives (to articulate the mix of competencies and levels of skills needed to improve productivity), but should also incorporate tertiary education leadership (to identify areas of comparative strength within the tertiary system). Although similar in their institutional cultures and internal organization, tertiary institutions serve their countries most effectively when each excels in a few strategic areas as members of a national innovation system (World Bank 2002). "A diverse tertiary system, with a variety of institutions pursuing different goals and student audiences, is best able to serve individual and national goals" (Task Force on Higher Education and Society 2000).

Implementation of human resource development strategies is likely to produce the best results when it is based on a positive incentive system that rewards the systemic changes desired (World Bank 2002). As one example, funding formulae are a transparent method for the universal application of a results-based approach to an entire tertiary system, rather than to individual institutions. They are currently employed in New Zealand, Poland, and South Africa, among others (Salmi and Hauptmann 2006). However, they have often proven difficult to introduce in developing countries, in part because of deficiencies in their management information systems and performance monitoring capacities (World Bank 2002). Alternatively, tertiary institutions can be individually funded on the basis of achieved results (rather than promised results) through institutional performance contracts. This method is currently used in Australia, Chile, and France, among others. Funding formulae and performance contracts work best where governments hold clear ideas regarding the needed path of reforms, and funding incentives can be employed to steer them in this direction.

Where there is need to unleash creative energies that improve upon existing ways of doing things, competitive funding mechanisms can be employed to good effect. These have been used successfully in numerous countries to encourage innovation in teaching, or to introduce a more strongly applied orientation to research (World Bank 2002; Fielden 2007; Saint 2006).[27] Personnel policies, such as promotion criteria, can also be enlisted to encourage innovation. Likewise, cash prizes might be awarded to recognize (and draw public attention to) special accomplishments. But these latter incentives work best when institutional management is vested with the autonomy to hire or fire staff, approve or deny promotions, and increase or decrease salaries in response to periodic reviews of staff performance.

- *Reform financing arrangements to offer incentives for attaining policy goals while providing the stability necessary for institutions to plan strategically.*

The task of funding tertiary education will become increasingly difficult in the years ahead. Each country will have to devise a financing approach that plays to its economic strengths, its institutional capacities, and its political possibilities. In doing so, various options may be considered, some of which are controversial. The share of government expenditures on basic education and tertiary education could be raised above current levels. Tuition and fees could be increased for students in public tertiary institutions, particularly where it is shown that they come from the country's richest households. Donor agencies, including the World Bank, could be asked to contribute more to secondary and tertiary education without reducing their commitments to basic education. Private provision of tertiary education could be encouraged to accommodate up to half of tertiary enrollments. Lower-cost delivery of tertiary education through innovative, flexible, ICT-supported arrangements could be explored. Off-shore educational providers—whether operating through local franchises, branch campuses, or distance education—could be invited to join the national tertiary education system in some countries, bringing with them possible sources of innovation in pedagogy, curriculum, and modes of delivery. Special earmarked taxes to support secondary or tertiary education could be introduced, as has been done in Ghana and Nigeria. Public-private partnerships could be developed in which local firms sponsor particular courses of study or fields of research that are of potential benefit to them, or contribute to a general development fund, as in Tanzania. And efficiency gains could be more aggressively pursued, particularly through a redirection of non-strategic overseas scholarship funds to boost the quality of national-level teaching, learning, and research.

In the end, however, governments are advised to tackle systemic and institutional reforms before seeking to increase funding (World Bank Institute 2007). After reviewing the evidence for a positive relationship between resources and educational quality, Hanushek and Woessmann (2007) conclude, "The overall finding is that simple resource policies—reducing class sizes, increasing teacher salaries, spending more on schools, and so forth—have little consistent impact on student performance when the institutional structure is not changed."

- *Grant institutional autonomy, buttressed by appropriate accountability mechanisms in order to increase opportunities for system differentiation and institutional innovation.*

The complementary presence of autonomy, accountability, and competition within tertiary education systems is necessary in order to foster quality. In their global analysis of education quality and economic growth, Hanushek and Woessmann (2007) also conclude that student learning performance is heavily dependent on three institutional features that must be combined in a single policy package in order to be effective: *competition and choice* among schools so that student demand will create performance incentives for individual schools; *autonomy* in decision making so that institutional managers and governing bodies can take the actions they see necessary to promote educational achievement; and an *accountability* system that identifies good school performance and leads to rewards based on this.

At the tertiary level, competition and choice are expressed in the diversity of prevailing institutional types and academic programs that comprise the system. Autonomy is embedded in the institutions' formal relation to the state, as expressed in the degree of local decision making and fiscal decentralization that a government is willing to permit, since these shape the institution's scope for flexibility and innovation. Accountability derives from stakeholder representation in institutional governance, from participatory strategic planning, and from the mechanisms put in place for quality assurance. In numerous African nations, one or more of these three essential elements may be underdeveloped or even lacking entirely.

The composition of tertiary governing councils often reflects degrees of autonomy and lines of accountability. Council composition displays widely differing patterns across Africa. In some cases, the bulk of the council's members are drawn from government. In other cases, internal interest groups from the institution (administrators, staff, employees, students) are strongly represented. However, recent tertiary education governance reforms have incorporated greater private sector expertise, and occasionally integrated distinguished leaders from tertiary education systems outside the country in the effort to access international experience.

- *Encourage a diversity of different teaching and learning techniques.*

Perhaps the most sizable test facing tertiary institutions in Africa as they attempt to usher in a culture favoring innovation is that of changing their traditional pedagogy. This will be particularly difficult because it involves a shift in the longstanding institutional culture with regard to what constitutes "teaching" and a "good teacher." The elements of this conversion are well known and are actively proselytized in education literature around the world: interdisciplinary rather than disciplinary perspectives, flexibility in learning, group work instead of lectures, problem solving rather than memorization of facts, practical learning (field trips, attachments, internships) as a complement to theory, learning assessment through project work (i.e., demonstrated competence) instead of multiple choice examinations, communication skills, and computer literacy (Hagmann and Almekinders 2003; Savery and Duffy 2001; World Bank Institute 2007). But these elements have yet to be brought together and infused with African culture in a way that creates an approach to the teaching of science and technology that is appropriate for the African classroom and addresses specific African needs such as entrepreneurship education (World Bank 2006).

- *Develope postgraduate programs to increase academic staff numbers and build research capacity.*

National R&D efforts are more likely to be sustainable when they are grounded in national postgraduate programs and the professional networks that emerge around them. This linkage has borne fruit in Brazil, Chile, and India, where coordinated government policy initially fostered master's (and subsequently PhD) programs, actively encouraged research, and tied these expanding research capacities to their national agricultural research programs (Eicher 2006). Here, also, competitive funding mechanisms are an effective means of developing programs of strength in postgraduate teaching and research (World Bank 2002; Saint 2006).[28] As a general guideline, postgraduate training should first be undertaken locally whenever possible. When this capacity is exhausted, preference may be given to training in advanced industrial countries, preferably for highly specialized skills, using whenever possible a "sandwich" approach to reduce the costs. The next option would be training in other developing countries that have developed good quality higher education systems, such as Brazil, India, Malaysia, and South Africa.

- *Search for lower-cost delivery alternatives for tertiary education.*

Traditional face-to-face models of delivering postsecondary education are expensive and can limit developing country capacities for further enrollment expansion. Both governments and households are approaching the limits of what they can reasonably contribute to the financing of tertiary education. Alternative, lower-cost delivery models are needed if educational access is to grow in the years ahead. Fortunately, the elements of such a transformation are becoming discernible. They include lifelong learning, ICT applications to education, on-line distance education, open source courses, self-paced learning, and educational gameware. The long-term challenge for Africa is to establish education and training systems based on learning needs rather than on student age, and to replace information-based, rote learning with educational practices that develop a learner's ability to learn, create, adapt, and apply knowledge.

This study has sought to demonstrate why tertiary education systems in Sub-Saharan Africa must become better aligned with national economic development and poverty reduction strategies, and has identified the benefits likely to be associated with such a shift in perspective. It argues that the time for this realignment is now, and that the window of opportunity for reaping the benefits of such an initiative is limited to the coming 10 years or so. In doing so, it recognizes that governments and individual tertiary institutions have undertaken considerable reform under difficult conditions during the past decade, and that the quest for improvements of all kinds in SSA tertiary education is on-going. Nevertheless, a greater sense of urgency and redoubled efforts need to be brought to this task at this point in time. To do otherwise is really not an option. The consequences of inadequate action on this front are likely to be a flood of students into increasingly dysfunctional institutions, graduates without viable work skills, an unending demand for funding that throws public budgets into disarray, high levels of graduate unemployment, increasing politicization of education and employment policies, and growing possibilities of political unrest and instability. Contemplating this possibility should provide SSA governments and their citizens with an incentive for action.

We have also argued that this alignment process is best undertaken by each country individually, in accordance with its limitations and possibilities, through a consultative strategizing process involving all stakeholders. This will not be easy. The education sector, and tertiary institutions in particular, are conservative systems that house deeply entrenched interests and discourage outside intervention. Thus, management of the process is just as important as the final result.

Notes

1. The author refers to this as "Mode 2" knowledge production.

2. Writing in the mid-1990s, before the advent of the knowledge society, Ajayi, Goma, and Johnson (1996, p. 173) note with prescience "a growing need to redefine the role of the African university so as to emphasize research, creativity and the generation of new knowledge."

3. These are the Australian Innovation Action Plan (2001); Chile's National Strategy on Innovation (2007); the Malaysia Knowledge-based Economy Master Plan (2006); and Spain's new Ministry of Science and Innovation (2008), which also includes higher education.

4. These are the Mozambique Science, Technology and Innovation Strategy (2006), the Rwanda National Science, Technology, Scientific Research, and Innovation Policy (2005), and the South African National R&D Strategy (2002).

5. A recent review observes that many of these policy statements show a tendency to imitate documents from other countries and appear to contain a high degree of similarity in content and emphasis (Mouton 2008, pp. 12–13).

6. Surprisingly, although ample statistics exist on household costs for educating each student in the household, and on aggregate private contributions by families to the overall education budget, information on what share of the household budget is spent on education is scarce and country specific. For example, in Kenya, 15 percent of nonfood expenditures by families (and 5 percent of total expenditures) goes for educational costs (World Bank 2004b, p. 63). In Lesotho, primary school expenses cost families 15 percent of household income for each child enrolled (World Bank 2005, p. 76).

7. In various countries, pressures to elevate technical institutes and polytechnics to university status have reduced the numbers of technical education institutions. This process began in 1992 when the United Kingdom awarded university titles to its polytechnics, and has continued in Australia, Finland, Kenya, New Zealand, South Africa, and elsewhere (University World News 2008a; 2008b; 2008c; 2008d).

8. Ireland began with seven, but now has 14 institutes of technology. Six out of every 10 Irish tertiary students major in engineering, science, or business studies (O'Hare 2006, p. 20).

9. Competency-based training shifts the learning emphasis from the number of courses taken by the trainee to what the trainee has actually learned to do. It is often modular in organization, and facilitates flexible entry and exit. Implementation is complex and must include the development of standards based on job analysis and new forms of student assessment.

10. The principal exceptions are Denmark, France, Germany, Japan, and Switzerland.

11. This is evident not only in OECD countries, but also in Brazil, China, and Malaysia, where government policy is being used to develop complex capacities for innovation (Bleiklie, Laredo, and Sorlin 2007).

12. A recent survey rated university autonomy as "high" in 13 of 23 European countries in that institutions are largely self-governing (Karran 2007). These include Austria, the Czech Republic, Estonia, Finland, Germany, Hungary, Italy, Latvia, Lithuania, Poland, Slovakia, Slovenia, and Spain. Notably, the Western notion of autonomy as independence from state intervention may not be appropriate for China because of its long tradition of co-opting scholars into government service (Pan 2007, p. 123).

13. Ten SSA Anglophone countries were included in a 1996 survey of institutional autonomy among universities in 27 countries of the British Commonwealth (Richardson and Fielden 1997). Based on a review of university acts and a 55-item questionnaire, an autonomy score was given to each country. The results showed Sub-Saharan Africa (10 countries) to be slightly below the Commonwealth mean, but enjoying greater autonomy than Commonwealth countries in the Mediterranean (two countries) and Asia (seven countries). This suggests that even before the governance reforms of the past decade, African universities were not significantly less autonomous than other Commonwealth institutions. This raises the question of whether African tertiary institutions need to be granted further autonomy, or whether they simply need to take fuller advantage of the autonomy they have already been given.

14. Stakeholders are normally considered to comprise government, civil society, academic staff, and students, but with the rise of globalization, the representatives of private enterprise have been increasingly recognized as a separate stakeholder group.

15. Malawi became the most recent member of this group in early 2008.

16. For those countries for which information is available on the International Association of Universities Web site, the average date of national higher education legislation in 12 Francophone countries is 1994, whereas the average date for nine Anglophone countries is 1998.

17. Reforms over the past decade in Australia, Denmark, New Zealand, and the United Kingdom have reduced governing board membership for universities to 10 to 12 persons (Fielden 2007, p. 42).

18. Where academic staff are little different from civil servants, where salary increases depend on years of service, where it is impossible to dismiss anyone for poor performance, and where political interference erodes institutional autonomy, academic mediocrity is almost guaranteed (Kapur and Crowley 2008, p. 43).

19. For example, the predominance of administrative personnel on institutional payrolls, which averages 60 percent in SSA Francophone countries (Brossard and Foko 2007).

20. Case studies of "things that work" in Africa's tertiary education formed the basis of the World Bank's 2003 regional conference, held in Accra, Ghana. See www.worldbank.org/afr/teia.

21. Countries with S&T enrollment shares in the 20 percent to 25 percent range include Australia, Chile, France, India, the United Kingdom, and the United States (UNESCO ISCED enrollment data).

22. Data from the UNESCO Institute for Statistics, although sketchy for graduate-level enrollments (ISCED Level 6) appear to show a decline from 2 percent to 1 percent of total enrollments since the year 2000.

23. One result of this approach would be to add prestige to the award of tenure and increase the competition for its attainment. Pakistan has recently taken this step as part of its tertiary education reform.

24. ANSTI provided more than 200 scholarships for graduate study within the region between 1994 and 2003 (www.ansti.org/index.php?option =com_content&task=blogsection&id=12&Itemid=46).

25. Information retrieved from: http://www.aims.ac.za/english/index.php.

26. Private universities account for 73 percent of higher education enrollments in Brazil, 71 percent in Chile, and 75 percent in Korea (PROPHE 2007; World Bank 2002, p. 71).

27. Competitive research funds have produced good capacity-building results in Chile, Brazil, India, Vietnam, and elsewhere; they are being introduced by Uganda. Mozambique and Nigeria have recently established national research funds to award competitive research grants.

28. Another alternative is to support regional postgraduate programs. For a detailed discussion on this issue, see Fine (2007) and Tongoona and Mudhara (2007).

Annex A

Private Colleges and Universities in Sub-Saharan Africa

Country	Number
Angola	7
Benin	27
Botswana	5
Burkina Faso	4
Burundi	2
Cameroon	13
Cape Verde	1
Central African Republic	4
Chad	2
Congo, Dem. Rep. of	39
Congo, Rep. of	4
Côte d'Ivoire	1
Eritrea	1
Ethiopia	12
Gabon	3
Gambia, The	0
Ghana	25
Guinea	1
Kenya	19
Lesotho	15

(continued)

Private Colleges and Universities in Sub-Saharan Africa (*continued*)

Country	Number
Liberia	3
Madagascar	16
Malawi	0
Mali	2
Mauritania	0
Mauritius	2
Mozambique	5
Namibia	1
Niger	0
Nigeria	34
Rwanda	12
Senegal	41
Sierra Leone	0
South Africa	79
Sudan	22
Swaziland	0
Tanzania	17
Togo	22
Uganda	23
Zambia	0
Zimbabwe	4
SSA	468
Francophone	*53%*
Anglophone	*34%*
Other	*13%*

Note: No comprehensive listing of private tertiary institutions yet exists in Sub-Saharan Africa. The data presented here are drawn from all available sources, including Teferra and Altbach (2003), World Bank data, newsletters, and newspapers. However, the results should only be considered an estimate.

Africa Region—New Commitments for Education by Subsector FY1990–2008

Sub-sector	FY90	FY91	FY92	FY93	FY94	FY95	FY96	FY97	FY98	FY99	FY00	FY01	FY02	FY03	FY04	FY05	FY06	FY07	FY08
									IBRD + IDA New Commitments (millions of current US$)										
Primary education	91	153	83	184	99	104	95	15	226	126	57	60	214	238	92	106	91	258	45
Secondary education	39	19	40	32	26	12	—	19	98	11	14	14	—	54	124	11	18	141	4
Tertiary education	**120**	**31**	**164**	**131**	**70**	**30**	**42**	**12**	**46**	**25**	**14**	**17**	**69**	**—**	**46**	**61**	**29**	**106**	**105**
Total	**250**	**203**	**287**	**347**	**195**	**146**	**137**	**46**	**370**	**162**	**85**	**91**	**283**	**292**	**262**	**178**	**138**	**505**	**154**

Source: World Bank data.

Africa Region—New Commitments for Education by Sub-Sector FY90–08
Three year Two-sided Moving Average (MA)

									IBRD + IDA New Commitments (millions of current US$)										
Sub-sector	FY90	FY91	FY92	FY93	FY94	FY95	FY96	FY97	FY98	FY99	FY00	FY01	FY02	FY03	FY04	FY05	FY06	FY07	FY08
Primary education	122	108	140	122	129	100	72	112	123	137	81	111	171	181	145	96	152	131	151
Secondary education	29	33	30	33	23	19	16	59	43	41	13	14	34	89	63	51	43	43	55
Tertiary education	**75**	**105**	**109**	**122**	**77**	**47**	**28**	**33**	**27**	**28**	**19**	**33**	**43**	**58**	**54**	**45**	**77**	**92**	**123**
Total	**226**	**246**	**279**	**277**	**229**	**166**	**116**	**204**	**193**	**206**	**113**	**158**	**248**	**328**	**262**	**192**	**272**	**266**	**329**

Source: Calculations based on World Bank data.

Annex B

Tertiary-Level Human Resource Skills Implications of 14 Current Poverty Reduction Strategy Papers (PRSPs)

Country	PRSP time period	Main objectives	Implications for tertiary-level human resource development
Burkina Faso	2005–2007	• Promote rural development and food security • Improve public access to safe drinking water • Combat HIV/AIDS • Protect the environment • Develop SMIs/SMEs and small-scale mining • Strengthen public safety • Enhance national capacities, with particular emphasis on new information and communications technologies	• Agricultural researchers (various disciplines); civil engineers and technicians; rural extensionists; agricultural engineers; irrigation specialists; vocational teachers • Civil engineers; topographers • Doctors; nurses; health educators; public health specialists; pharmacologists and technicians; hematologists • Environmentalists (various disciplines); natural resource management; environmental education • Business education; accounting; finance; mining engineers • Highway engineers; road maintenance technicians • Electrical engineers; electrical and computer technicians; telecommunications; ICT instructors
Burundi	2007–2009	• Improve governance and security • Promote sustainable and equitable economic growth • Develop human capital • Prevent and control HIV/AIDS	• Public administration; professionalized police and military; forestry; civil engineering; lawyers; judges; prison administration • Land management; land-use planning; surveying; rural finance; agricultural production (paddy rice, coffee, tea, cotton, wheat, maize, beans, cassava, bananas); food technology; livestock production; aquaculture; natural resource management; business and finance; mining engineers and technicians; tourism and hotel administration; road engineers and maintenance technicians • Electrical engineers and technicians; computer technicians; telecommunications; ICT instructors; teacher educators; education managers; vocational teachers; water and sanitation • Doctors; nurses; health educators; public health specialists; AIDS counselors; pharmacologists and technicians

Chad	2004–2015	• Promote good governance • Ensure economic growth • Improve human capital • Reduce poverty for vulnerable groups (health, education, roads, rural development) • Restore and safeguard the ecosystem	• Public administration; law and judiciary • Economists; petroleum engineering and technology; cotton production and textiles; environmental safety; finance • Civil engineering, mechanical engineering, electrical engineering; engineering technicians; alternative energy technicians; telecommunications; finance; accounting; business education; vocational education • Doctors; nurses; health educators; public health specialists; AIDS counselors; pharmacologists and technicians; teacher educators; education managers • Environmental regulation; environmental education; natural resource management
Congo, Dem. Rep. of	2007–2009	• Promote good governance and consolidate peace (through strengthened institutions) • Consolidate macroeconomic stability and growth • Improve access to social services (roads, education, health, water and sanitation) • Combat HIV/AIDS • Promote local initiatives	• Public administration; law and judiciary; tax law and administration; customs administration; accounting; professionally trained security forces • Macroeconomics; statistics; demography; seed production (cotton, potatoes, vegetables); livestock production; extension; marketing; credit and finance; forestry; mining technology • Highway engineers and technicians; teacher educators; sanitary engineers; waste management; electrical engineers and technicians; vocational/technical education; distance education; telecommunications • Doctors; nurses; health educators; public health specialists; AIDS counselors • Project planning and management; community finance

(continued)

121

Tertiary-Level Human Resource Skills Implications of 14 Current Poverty Reduction Strategy Papers (PRSPs) *(continued)*

Country	PRSP time period	Main objectives	Implications for tertiary-level human resource development
Ethiopa	2003–2006	• Intentional focus on agriculture as initial source of economic growth • Strengthen private sector • Promote high-value agricultural exports, particularly quality leather and textile garments • Expand education and human resource development • Deepen the governmental decentralization process and improve governance	• Agricultural research and extension; seed production; livestock production; water resources management; irrigation construction and management; vocational and technical teacher training; cooperatives and marketing • Livestock nutrition and health; leather processing technologies; cotton production; textile technologies • Export promotion; tax and customs administration; land-use planning; finance; accounting • Teacher education; technical education; higher education leadership and management; public health specialists; doctors; nurses; civil engineers; sanitation engineers • Public administration; civic education; disaster preparedness and response
Ghana	2006–2009	• Prioritize human resource development • Modernize agriculture • Foster new growth sectors • Develop the private sector	• Teacher education; vocational and technical education; science education; distance education; education managers; doctors; nurses; public health specialists; demographers; sanitary engineers; urban development • Research and technology capacities linked to cocoa and tropical fruit exports; aquaculture; water resources management; seed production; extension personnel; refrigeration technicians; civil engineers; agricultural engineers; agricultural processing technologists; natural resource management and conservation • Tourism management; hotel management; textile designers; industrial engineers; mining engineers; ICT technicians; film arts • Business educators; lawyers; finance; accountants; trade promotion; weights and standards setting; electrical engineers

Kenya	2003–2007	• Create conditions for growth • Rehabilitate and maintain infrastructure • Improve access to basic education and health services • Develop agriculture of arid and semiarid areas • Upgrade living conditions for urban poor • Strengthen rule of law and security • Strengthen capacities for public administration	• Financial planning and management; tax administration; public administration; banking; port management; sustainable energy sources; hotel/hospitality management • Civil engineers; road maintenance technicians; water resource management; transportation planners; civil aviation; telecommunications; ICT technicians; aircraft maintenance • Teacher education; doctors; nurses; public health specialists; pharmacologists; pharmacy technicians • Irrigation engineering; natural resource management; agricultural research; agricultural extension; rural finance; agricultural processing and storage; veterinary medicine • Sanitation engineers; waste management technicians • Security planning and management; police training • Database management; computer technicians; software engineers; judicial administration; contract law; marine resource planning and management; pension management
Madagascar	2007–2012	• Responsible governance • Connected infrastructure • Educational transformation • Rural development and a green revolution • Health, family planning, and HIV/AIDS • High-growth economy • Cherish the environment • National solidarity	• Lawyers; legal assistants; professional security managers; human rights education; tax administration; public administration • Port management; transportation planning; highway maintenance; project management; civil engineering; public safety; electrical engineering; alternative energy; thermal power; ICT technicians; telecommunications; meteorology; water and sanitation systems • Teacher educators; curriculum planners; pedagogy specialists; education management; librarians; vocational and technical teachers; ICT instructors; management information systems; distance education; academic staff for graduate teaching

(continued)

Tertiary-Level Human Resource Skills Implications of 14 Current Poverty Reduction Strategy Papers (PRSPs) (continued)

Country	PRSP time period	Main objectives	Implications for tertiary-level human resource development
			• Surveyors; land law; management information systems; rural finance; irrigation engineering; seed production; agricultural engineering; rice production; agricultural extension; agribusiness • Doctors; nurses; public health specialists; pharmacology; health economists; family planning specialists; STD specialists; hematology; epidemiology; obstetrics; gynecology; nutritionists • Finance; insurance; statistics; vocational and technical education; banking; trade policy; trade law; macroeconomics; natural resources management; mining engineering; hotel and hospitality management; advertising • Environmental conservation, cartography; resource economics; forestry; soil sciences; environmental planning; regulatory law • Civic education; fine arts; disaster preparedness; women's rights law
Mali	2002–2025	• Institutional development and improved governance • Human resources development and access to basic services • Infrastructure and productive sector development	• Public administration; law and judicial administration; macroeconomics; public security planning and management; human resources management; tourism management; development planning; management information systems; investigative journalism; auditing • Teacher education; doctors, nurses, hospital administration; maternal/child health; health regulations and monitoring; nutrition; hematology; pharmacology; family planning; water supply and sanitation engineering; vocational and technical education; psychology; social insurance

		• Energy development and management; road construction and maintenance; agricultural sciences (cotton, rice, livestock, poultry, horticulture); soil sciences; finance; banking; market development; trade policy; transportation planning; telecommunications; natural resource management; irrigation engineering; hydrology; surveyors and land titling; tourism planning and management
Mozambique	2006–2009	• Improve governance, administration of justice, and rule of law • Expand human capital and raise quality • Provide supportive environment for economic development	• Public administration; human rights law; judicial administration; public finance; management information systems; human resource management; tax administration; audit and accounting; prison administration; police training • Teacher educators; vocational and technical education; agricultural sciences; health sciences; education planning and management; special education; primary health care; reproductive health; maternal/child health; pediatrics; hematology; pharmacology; nutrition; public health specialists; epidemiology; water and sanitation; hydrology; meteorology; physical education; construction technology • Tax administration; macroeconomics; microeconomics; public finance; accounting; banking; insurance; labor law; social insurance; electrical engineering; alternative energy sources; telecommunications; ICT technicians; agricultural research and extension; seed production; plant and livestock sanitation; agribusiness; natural resources management; fisheries; forestry; tourism planning and management; geology; mining engineering; trade policy; port administration

(continued)

Tertiary-Level Human Resource Skills Implications of 14 Current Poverty Reduction Strategy Papers (PRSPs) *(continued)*

Country	PRSP time period	Main objectives	Implications for tertiary-level human resource development
Rwanda	2003–2006	• Rural development and agricultural transformation • Increased human development • Improved economic infrastructure • Enhanced governance • Private sector development • Institutional capacity building	• Soil sciences; natural resource management; agricultural research and extension (rice, maize, potatoes, soya, beans, coffee); seed production; rural finance; livestock production; marketing/storage of agricultural products • Public health specialists; maternal/child health; health services management; hematology; pharmacology; water and sanitation; health education; family planning; teacher education; curriculum development; science education; distance education; applied technology research; ICT technicians; technical education; scholarships for women • Land-use planning; construction technology; alternative energy sources; electrical engineering; highway engineering and road maintenance; telecommunications • Conflict resolution and mediation; human rights and civic education; administration of justice; prison management; public finance; public administration; audit and accounting • Business and finance; banking; commercial law; mining law tourism planning and management; ICT technicians • Social insurance; human resource management; land law, titling, registry management

	2006–2010	• Wealth creation for pro-poor growth • Expanded access to basic social services • Social protection and disaster preparedness • Decentralized governance	• Natural resource management; soil sciences; entomology; land-use planning; forestry; hydrology and irrigation engineering; agricultural research and extension (sesame, asparagus); seed production; agricultural engineering; organic standards and certification; agribusiness; livestock production and sanitation; rural finance; fisheries; geology; mining technology; environmental conservation; trade policy; tourism planning and management; ICT technicians; telecommunications; transportation planning; road maintenance; alternative energy sources; electrical engineering; tax administration • Teacher education; special education; education planning and management; vocational and technical education; health systems management; public health specialists; maternal/child health; hematology; epidemiology; water and sanitation • Social insurance; disaster planning; risk insurance; special education; family planning • Public finance; tax administration; human resource management; administration of justice; strategic planning and implementation; management information systems
Senegal			
Tanzania	2006–2010	• Economic growth and poverty reduction • Improved quality of life and social well-being • Improved governance and accountability	• Macroeconomics; trade policy; public finance; civic engineering; road maintenance; entomology; livestock production and sanitation; mining law; mining technology; agricultural research and extension; agribusiness and processing technology; small business development; forestry; fisheries; vocational and technical education; electrical engineering; petroleum engineering

(continued)

Tertiary-Level Human Resource Skills Implications of 14 Current Poverty Reduction Strategy Papers (PRSPs) *(continued)*

Country	PRSP time period	Main objectives	Implications for tertiary-level human resource development
			• Teacher education; curriculum development (with gender sensitivity); educational planning and management; maternal/child health; nutrition; public health specialists; hematology; pharmacology; nursing; health systems management; family planning; human resource management; water supply; sanitation and waste management; land titling and records; environmental conservation; natural resource management; social insurance; social work
			• Public finance; public administration; human resource management; investigative journalism; civil law, human rights, and legal assistance; administration of justice; legal recourse for physically and mentally challenged persons; police training
Uganda	2005–2008	• Strengthen economic management	• Public finance; tax administration; macroeconomics; pension management
		• Enhance production, competitiveness, and incomes	• Trade policy; agricultural research and extension; meteorology; livestock production, agricultural education; water resource management; irrigation engineering; land-use planning; land titling and registry; fisheries management; management information systems; forestry; business education; tourism planning and management; mining law; road construction and maintenance; electrical engineering; airport management
		• Improve security and conflict management	• Refugee assistance, planning, and management
		• Advance good governance	• Human rights education; administration of justice; juvenile justice; commercial law; dispute resolution; legal assistance; audit and accounting; public sector ethics; human resource management
		• Expand human development	• Teacher education; special education; curriculum reform; learning assessment; guidance and counseling; science education; vocational and technical education; doctors; nurses; public health specialists; maternal/child health; pharmacology; family planning; water and sanitation

Source: Poverty Reduction Strategy Papers (PRSPs), The World Bank, 2008.

Annex C

Regional Postgraduate Programs in Sub-Saharan Africa

Name of Program	Lead institution	Discipline	Level
African Centre for Crop Improvement	University of KwaZulu-Natal, South Africa	Plant breeding and biotechnology	PhD
African Economic Research Consortium	AERC Secretariat, Nairobi, Kenya	Economics	MA, PhD
African Regional Postgraduate Programme in Insect Science	International Centre of Insect Physiology and Ecology (ECIPE)	Entomology	MS, PhD
Agribusiness	Africa University, Mutare, Zimbabwe	Agricultural economics	MS

(continued)

Regional Postgraduate Programs in Sub-Saharan Africa (*continued*)

Name of program	Lead institution	Discipline	Level
Agricultural information and communications management	Haromaya University, Ethiopia; Makerere University, Uganda; Sokoine University, Tanzania; University of Nairobi, Kenya	Agriculture	MS
Aquaculture and fisheries science	University of Malawi	Fisheries	MS, PhD
Agricultural and resource economics	University of Malawi	Agricultural economics	MS, PhD
ANSTI Water Resources Engineering	University of Dar es Salaam, Tanzania	Engineering and environment	MS, PhD
Biotechnology and plant breeding	Makerere University, Uganda	Crop production	MS, PhD
Building Africa's Scientific and Institutional Capacity in Agriculture and Natural Resources (BASIC)	Forum for Agricultural Research in Africa (FARA),	Various	MS, PhD
Collaborative Master of Science in Agricultural and Applied Economics (CMAAE)	Nairobi Kenya	Agricultural economics	MS
Dairy science and technology	University of Zimbabwe	Animal production	MS
Dryland resource management	University of Nairobi, Kenya	Natural resource management	MS, PhD
Food science and nutrition	Jomo Kenyatta University of Agriculture and Technology, Kenya	Food technology	MS, PhD
General agriculture	University of the Free State,	Agriculture	MS

(continued)

Regional Postgraduate Programs in Sub-Saharan Africa (*continued*)

Name of program	Lead institution	Discipline	Level
Plant breeding and biotechnology	African Center for Crop Improvement, University of KwaZulu-Natal, South Africa	Crop production	PhD
Plant breeding and seed systems	University of Zambia	Crop production	MS
Regional Universities Forum for Capacity Building in Agriculture (RUFORUM)	Makerere University, Kampala, Uganda	Various	MS, Developing PhD
Research methodology	Jomo Kenyatta University of Agriculture and Technology, Kenya; University of Malawi	Agriculture	MS
Sasakawa Africa Fund for Extension Education	Bunda, Univ. of Cape Coast	Extension education	MS
Southern African Center for Cooperation in Agricultural and Natural Resources Research and Training (SACCAR)	(Four participating universities)	Animal science- crop science Agricultural economics Agricultural engineering and irrigation	MS MS MS MS
University Science, Humanities and Engineering Partnerships in Africa (USHEPiA)	University of Cape Town, South Africa	Science and engineering	MS, PhD
United Methodist Church University in Africa	Africa University, Mutare, Zimbabwe	Agriculture and other disciplines	MS

Source: Calculations based on World Bank data.

Annex D

Estimated Unit Recurrent Expenditure per Student in SSA Tertiary Education, 2006

Country	US$
Benin	864
Burkina Faso	3,192
Burundi	5,893
Cameroon	864
Central African Republic	864
Chad	1,584
Congo, Dem. Rep. of	286
Congo, Rep. of	1,900
Côte d'Ivoire	957
Eritrea	860
Ethiopia	2,016
Gambia, The	1,102
Ghana	1,924
Guinea	615
Kenya	1,508
Lesotho	7,742
Madagascar	588
Malawi	2,533
Mali	836

(continued)

**Estimated Unit Recurrent Expenditure per Student in SSA
Tertiary Education, 2006 (*continued*)**

Country	US$
Mauritania	666
Mozambique	2,244
Niger	1,482
Nigeria	704
Rwanda	1,975
Senegal	2,100
Sierra Leone	816
Sudan	891
Tanzania	1,855
Togo	455
Uganda	570
Zambia	1,827
Zimbabwe	782

Sources: Authors calculations based on Ledoux and Mingat 2008; World Bank 2008.

References

Acemoglu, Daron. 2002. "Directed Technical Change." *Review of Economic Studies* 69 (4): 781–809.

Acemoglu, Daron, and Fabrizio Zilibotti. 2001. "Productivity Differences." *Quarterly Journal of Economics* 116 (2): 563–606.

Adams, Richard H. Jr. 2006. "International Remittances and the Household: Analysis and Review of Global Evidence." *Journal of African Economies* 15 (S2): 396–425.

African Network of Scientific and Technical Institutions (ANSTI). 2005a. "Revitalizing Science and Technology Training Institutions in Africa: The Way Forward." Presented at The First African Conference of Vice-Chancellors, Provosts and Deans of Science, Engineering and Technology, Accra, Ghana, November 15.

———. 2005b. *The State of Science and Technology Training Institutions in Africa.* Nairobi, Kenya: UNESCO (United Nations Educational, Scientific and Cultural Organization).

Afrozone. 2005. "Training Needs Assessments, Job Market Surveys, and Tracer Studies," Sokoine University of Agriculture, Morogoro, Tanzania.

Agarwal, Pawan. 2006. "Higher Education in India: The Need for Change." Working paper 180. Indian Council for Research on International Economic Relations, New Delhi.

Aggarwal, Reena, Asli Demirguc-Kunt, and Maria Soledad Martinez Peria. 2006. "Do Worker's Remittances Promote Financial Development?" World Bank Policy Research Working Paper 3957, World Bank, Washington, DC.

Aghion, Philippe, Leah Boustan, Caroline Hoxby, and Jerome Vandenbussche. 2005. "Exploiting States' Mistakes to Identify the Causal Impact of Higher Education on Growth," Harvard University, Cambridge, MA.

Agrisystems (Eastern Africa). 2005. "Future Opportunities and Challenges for Agricultural Learning (Focal) Programme: Job Market Survey, Training Needs Assessment and Tracer Studies" for Sokoine University of Agriculture in Veterinary Medicine and Animal Science. Sokoine University of Agriculture, Morogoro, Tanzania.

Ajayi, J.F. Ade, Lameck K.H. Goma, and G. Ampah Johnson. 1996. *The African Experience with Higher Education.* London: James Currey Ltd.

Al-Samarrai, Samer, and Paul Bennell. 2003. "Where Has All the Education Gone in Africa? Employment Outcomes Among Secondary School and University Leavers," Institute of Development Studies, University of Sussex, Brighton, UK.

Altbach, Philip G. 2005a. "Private Higher Education: An Introduction." In *Private Higher Education: A Global Revolution*, ed. Philip G. Altbach and Daniel C. Levy. Rotterdam, the Netherlands: Sense Publishers.

———. 2005b. "The Anatomy of Private Higher Education." In *Private Higher Education: A Global Revolution*, ed. Philip G. Altbach and Daniel C. Levy. Rotterdam, the Netherlands: Sense Publishers.

———. 2007. "Peripheries and Centres: Research Universities in Developing Countries." *Higher Education Management and Policy* 19 (2): 106–30.

Amelewonou, K., and M. Brossard. 2005. "Développer L'Éeducation Secondaire En Afrique: Enjeux, Contraintes Et Marges De Manoeuvre." Presented at l'Atelier regional sur l'éducation secondaire en Afrique, Addis Ababa, Ethiopia, November 21.

Aromolaran, Adebayo B. 2006. "Estimates of Mincerian Returns to Schooling in Nigeria." *Oxford Development Studies* 34 (2): 265–92.

Artadi, Elsa V., and Xavier Sala-i-Martin. 2003. "The Economic Tragedy of the XXth Century: Growth in Africa." NBER Working Paper 9865, National Bureau of Economic Research, Cambridge, MA.

Association of African Universities. 2007. *HIV & AIDS and Higher Education in Africa: A Review of Best Practices Models and Trends.* Accra, Ghana: Association of African Universities.

Association of Commonwealth Universities. 2006. "The World Is One: Mobilising the Capacity of Tertiary Education in the Commonwealth for the Good of All." Presented at the 16th Conference of Commonwealth Ministers of Education, Cape Town, South Africa, December 11–14.

Atefi, George, personal communication, 2008.

Autor, David H., Frank Levy, and Richard J. Murnane. 2001. "The Skill Content of Recent Technological Change: An Empirical Exploration." NBER Working Paper 8337, National Bureau of Economic Research, Cambridge, MA.

Azam, Jean-Paul, and Flore Gubert. 2006. "Migrants' Remittances and the Household in Africa: A Review of Evidence." *Journal of African Economies* 15 (S2): 426–62.

Azcona, Ginette, Rachel Chute, Farah Dib, Loveena Dookhony, Heather Klein, Daniel Loyacano-Perl, Dominic Randazzo, and Vanessa Reilly. 2008. "Harvesting the Future: The Case for Tertiary Education in Sub-Saharan Africa." The Maxwell School of Syracuse University, Syracuse, NY.

Barro, Robert J. and Jong-Wha Lee. 2000. "International Data on Educational Attainment: Updates and Implications." CID Working Paper 042. Cambridge, MA: Center for International Development, Harvard University.

Barro, Robert J., and Xavier Sala-i-Martin. 1995. *Economic Growth*. New York: McGraw-Hill.

Bates, Robert H., John H. Coatsworth, and Jeffrey G. Williamson. 2006. "Lost Decades: Lessons From Post-Independence Latin America for Today's Africa." NBER Working Paper 12610, National Bureau of Economic Research, Cambridge, MA.

Beck, Thorsten, and Ross Levine. 2002. "Industry Growth and Capital Allocation: Does Having a Market- or Bank-Based System Matter?" NBER Working Paper 8982, National Bureau of Economic Research, Cambridge, MA.

Beintema, Nienke, and Gert-Jan Stads. 2006. "Agricultural R&D in Sub-Saharan Africa: An Era of Stagnation." Agricultural Science & Technology Indicators (ASTI) background paper, International Food Policy Research Institute, Washington, DC.

Bigsten, Arne, Paul Collier, Stefan Dercon, Bernard Gauthier, Jan Willem Gunning, Anders Isaksson, Abena Oduro, Remco Oostendorp, Cathy Pattilo, Måns Söderbom, Michel Sylvain, Francis Teal, and Albert Zeufack. 1999. "Investment in Africa's Manufacturing Sector: A Four Country Panel Data Analysis." *Oxford Bulletin of Econoimcs and Statistics* 61 (4): 489–512.

Bils, Mark, and Peter Klenow. 2000. "Does Schooling Cause Growth?" *American Economic Review* 90 (5): 1160–83.

Birnbaum, R. 1983. *Maintaining Diversity in Higher Education*. San Francisco: Jossey-Bass.

Bladh, Agneta. 2007. "Institutional Autonomy With Increasing Dependency on Outside Actors." *Higher Education Policy* 20 (4): 243–59.

Bleiklie, Ivar, and Maurice Kogan. 2007. "Organization and Governance of Universities." *Higher Education Policy* 20 (4): 477–93.

Bleiklie, Ivar, Philippe Laredo, and Sverker Sorlin. 2007. "Conclusion: Emerging Patterns in Higher Education Systems." *Higher Education Policy* 20 (4): 495–500.

Bloom, David E., David Canning, and Kevin Chan. 2006a. "Higher Education and Economic Development." World Bank Working Paper 102, Africa Human Development Series, Washington, DC.

———. 2006b. "Higher Education and Economic Development in Africa," Harvard University, Cambridge, MA.

Bloom, David E., Matthew Hartley, and Henry Rosovsky. 2006. "Beyond Private Gain: The Public Benefits of Higher Education." In *International Handbook of Higher Education*, ed. James F. Forest and Philip G. Altbach. Dordrecht, the Netherlands: Springer Netherlands.

Boarini, Romina, and Hubert Strauss. 2007. "The Private Internal Rates of Return to Tertiary Education: New Estimates for 21 OECD Countries." OECD Economics Department Working Paper 591, Organisation for Economic Co-operation and Development, Paris.

Boateng, Kwabia, and E. Ofori-Sarpong. 2002. "An Analytical Study of the Labour Market for Graduates in Ghana," National Council for Tertiary Education, Accra, Ghana.

Brenton, Paul, and Mombert Hoppe. 2007. "Clothing and Export Diversification: Still a Route to Growth for Low Income Countries?" World Bank, Washington, DC.

Brimble, Peter, and Richard F. Doner. 2007. "University-Industry Linkages and Economic Development: The Case of Thailand." *World Development* 35 (6): 1021–36.

Brito, Lidia. 2003. "The Mozambican Experience in Initiating and Sustaining Tertiary Education Reform." Presented at the Africa Regional Training Conference, Improving Tertiary Education in Sub-Saharan Africa: Things That Work! Accra, Ghana, September 23.

Broadman, Harry G. 2007. "Connecting Africa and Asia." *Finance and Development* 44 (2). http://www.imf.org/external/pubs/ft/fandd/2007/06/broadman.htm.

Brossard, Mathieu, and Borel Foko. 2006. L'Enseignement Supérieur En Afrique Francophone: Coúts Et Financement Et Perspectives De Développement Dans Une Logique De Soutenabilité Budgétaire, UNESCO-BREDA, Dakar, Senegal.

———. 2007. *Coûts Et Financement De L'Enseignement Supérieur En Afrique Francophone*. World Bank, Washington, DC.

Bruns, Barbara, Alain Mingat, and Ramahatra Rakotomalala. 2003. *Achieving Universal Primary Education by 2015: A Chance for Every Child*. Washington, DC: World Bank.

Budree, Reena. 2006. "Academic Staff Retention Survey," University of KwaZulu-Natal, Durban, South Africa.

Bunwaree, Sheila, and Sanjeev K. Sobhee. 2007. "University-Industry Linkages: The Case of Mauritius," World Bank, Washington, DC.

Butagira, Tabu, and Agness Nandutu. 2008. "All University Staff to Lose Permanent Jobs." *The Monitor* (Feb. 26).

Caesar, William K., Riese Jens, and Thomas Seitz. 2007. "Betting on Biofuels." *The McKinsey Quarterly* (June 6). http://www.mckinseyquarterly.com/Energy_Resources_Materials/Strategy_Analysis/Betting_on_biofuels_1992_abstract?gp=1

Calderisi, Robert. 2006. *The Trouble With Africa: Why Foreign Aid Isn't Working.* New York: Palgrave Macmillan.

Calderon, Cesar. 2008. "Infrastructure and Growth in Africa." Presented at the World Bank, Washington, DC, April 3.

Carnoy, Martin. 2006. "Higher Education and Economic Development: India, China and the 21st Century." Paper presented at the Pan Asia Conference: Focus on Economic Challenges, Stanford Center for International Development, Stanford University, Palo Alto, CA, May 31–June 3.

Chami, Ralph, Connel Fullenkamp, and Samir Jahjah. 2005. "Are Immigrant Remittance Flows a Source of Capital for Development?" *IMF Staff Papers* 52 (1): 55–82.

Chandra, Vandana, Jessica Boccardo, and I. Osorio. 2007. "Export Diversification and Competitiveness in Developing Countries," World Bank, Washington, DC.

China Daily. 2006. "Scholarships for Africans Set to Double," November 3.

Cincotta, Richard. 2005. "State of the World 2005 Global Security Brief #2: Youth Bulge, Underemployment Raise Risks of Civil Conflict." WorldWatch Institute. http://www.worldwatch.org/node/76.

Cohen, Daniel, and Marcelo Soto. 2007. "Growth and Human Capital: Good Data, Good Results." *Journal of Economic Growth* 12 (1): 51–76.

Collier, Paul. 2007. *The Bottom Billion: Why the Poorest Countries Are Failing and What Can Be Done About It.* New York: Oxford University Press.

Commission for Africa. 2005. *Our Common Interest.* London: Commission for Africa.

Conley, Dalton, Gordon C. McCord, and Jeffrey D. Sachs. 2007. "Africa's Lagging Demographic Transition: Evidence From Exogenous Impacts of Malaria Ecology and Agricultural Technology." NBER Working Paper 12892. National Bureau of Economic Research, Cambridge, MA.

Connell, John, Pascal Zurn, Barbara Stilwell, Magda Awases, and Jean-Marc Braichet. 2007. "Sub-Saharan Africa: Beyond the Health Worker Migration Crisis?" *Social Science & Medicine* 64 (9): 1876–91.

Cooper, Frederick. 2002. *Africa Since 1940*. Cambridge, UK: Cambridge University Press.

Council of Economic Advisors. 2007. *Economic Report of the President*. Washington, DC: United States Government Printing Office.

Court, David. 1999. "Financing Higher Education in Africa: Makerere, the Quiet Revolution." Working paper 22883, World Bank, Washington, DC.

Crafts, Nicholas. 2007. "Recent European Economic Growth: Why Can't It Be Like the Golden Age?" *National Institute Economic Review* 199 (1): 69–81.

Dang, Hai-Anh, and F. Halsey Rogers. 2008. "How to Interpret the Growing Phenomenon of Private Tutoring: Human Capital Deepening, Inequality Increasing, or Waste of Resources?" World Bank Policy Research Working Paper 4530, World Bank, Washington, DC.

Daniel, John. 2007. Report of the Visitation Panel to the University of Ghana, Commonwealth of Learning, Vancouver, BC. http://www.col.org/colweb/webdav/site/myjahiasite/shared/docs/UofGhana_no%20picsweb.pdf

de Ferranti, David, Guillermo E. Perry, Indermit S. Gill, J. Luis Guasch, William F. Maloney, Carolina Sanchez-Paramo, and Norbert Schady. 2003. *Closing the Gap in Education and Technology*. Washington, DC: World Bank.

Devarajan, Shantayanan, William Easterly, and Howard Pack. 2002. "Low Investment Is Not the Constraint on African Development," Economic Development and Culturaly Change 51 (3): 547–571.

Development Associates. 2005. Focal Programme: Training Needs Assessment, Job Market Surveys and Tracer Studies for SUA Degree Programmes, Sokoine University of Agriculture, Morogoro, Tanzania.

Docquier, Frederic, and Abdeslam Marfouk. 2005. "International Migration by Educational Attainment: 1990–2000." World Bank Policy Research Working Paper 3382, World Bank, Washington, DC.

Dobson, Ian. 2008. "Finland: Polytechnics That Call Themselves Universities," *University World News*. April 13.

Dutta, Puja Vasudeva. 2006. "Returns to Education: New Evidence for India, 1983–1999." *Education Economics* 14 (4): 431–51.

Easterlin, Richard A. 1981. "Why Isn't the Whole World Developed?" *The Journal of Economic History* 41 (1): 1–19.

Economic Commission for Africa. 1985. "Mbabane Programme of Action: The Response of the African Institutions of Higher Learning to Africa's Rapidly Deteriorating Economic and Social Conditions." Presented at the Third Conference of Vice-Chancellors, Presidents and Rectors of Institutions of Higher Learning, Mbabane, Swaziland.

Economist. 2007. "Drying Up and Flooding Out," May 10.

———. 2008a. "Cereal Offenders," March 27.

———. 2008b. "Food for Thought," March 27.

———. 2008c. "Killing the Pampas's Golden Calf," March 27.

———. 2008d. "Needed: A New Revolution," March 27.

Economist Intelligence Unit. 2006a. "Africa's Economic Prospects," *Business Africa*, October 1.

———. 2006b. "Half and Half," *Business Africa*, November 1.

———. 2006c. "Oiling Palms," *Business Africa*, November 16.

———. 2006d. "Slipping," *Business Africa*, November 1.

———. 2007a. "No Export Guarantees," *Business Africa*, February 16.

———. 2007b. "Driving Growth," *Business Africa*, February 1.

Edwards, Sebastian. 2007. "Crises and Growth: A Latin American Perspective." NBER Working Paper 13019, National Bureau of Economic Research, Cambridge, MA.

Eicher, Carl K. 2006. "The Evolution of Agricultural Education and Training: Global Insights," World Bank, Washington, DC.

Eicher, Carl K., Karim Maredia, and Idah Sithole-Niang. 2006. "Crop Biotechnology and the African Farmer." *Foreign Policy* 31 (6): 504–27.

Eisemon, Thomas, and Jamil Salmi. 1993. "African Universities and the State: Prospects for Reform in Senegal and Uganda." *Higher Education* 25 (2): 151–68.

Ekong, Donald, and Patricia Plante. 1996. *Strategic Planning at Selected African Universities*. Accra, Ghana: Association of African Universities.

Essegbey, George O. 2007. University-Industry Linkages in Africa: The Ghana Case Study, World Bank, Washington, DC.

Etzkowitz, Henry, and Loet Leydesdorff. 1998. "The Endless Transition: a 'Triple Helix' of University-Industry-Government Relations." *Minerva* 36 (3): 203–08.

Fafchamps, Marcel and Remco Oostendorp. 2002. "Investment." In *Industrial Change in Africa: Micro Evidence on Zimbabwean Firms Under Structural Adjustment*, ed. Jan Willem Gunning and Remco Oostendorp, 153–186. New York: McMillian.

Federal Ministry of Education. 2007. *Nigerian Education Sector 10-Year Transformation Blueprint: 2006–2015*. Abuja, Nigeria: Federal Ministry of Education.

Fielden, John. 2007. "Global Trends in University Governance." Education Working Paper Series 9, World Bank, Washington, DC.

Fielden, John, and Norman LaRocque. 2008. "The Evolving Regulatory Context for Private Education in Emerging Economies," World Bank and International Financial Corporation, Washington, DC.

Financial Times. 2006. "African Infrastructure," November 21.

————. 2007a. "Chinese Set to Quadruple Agri-Biotech Spending," March 16.

————. 2007b. "Africa Urged to Boost Spending to Fight Malaria," March 14.

————. 2008. "Precious Grains," April 14.

————. 2008. "The End of Abundance," June 1.

Fine, Jeffrey. 2007. "Regional Mechanisms for Supporting Research and Development in Developing Countries." Presented at the Global Forum: Building Science, Technology, and Innovation Capacity for Sustainable Development and Poverty Reduction, Washington, DC, February 13.

Foster, A. D., and Mark R. Rosenzweig. 1996. "Technical Change and Human Capital Returns and Investments: Evidence From the Green Revolution." *American Economic Review* 86 (4): 931–53.

Freeman, Richard B., and David L. Lindauer. 1999. "Why Not Africa?" NBER Working Paper 6942, National Bureau of Economic Research, Cambridge, MA.

Fried, Jochen, Anna Glass, and Bernd Baumgartl. 2007. "Shades of Privateness: Non-Public Higher Education in Europe." In *The Rising Role and Relevance of Private Higher Education in Europe*, ed. P.J. Wells, J. Sadlak, and L. Vlasceanu. Bucharest, Romania: UNESCO-CEPES.

Fry, Peter, and Rogerio Utui. 1999. *Promoting Access, Quality and Capacity-Building in Africa Higher Education: The Strategic Planning Experience at the Equardo Mondlane University*. Washington, DC: World Bank.

Fung, Victor K., William K. Fung, and Yoram Wind. 2008. *Competing in a Flat World: Building Enterprises for a Borderless World*. Upper Saddle River, NJ: Pearson Education Inc.

Gaillard, J., and R. Waast. 2001. *Science in Africa at the Dawn of the 21st Century*. Paris: L'institut de recherché pour le développement.

Gans, Joshua S., and Scott Stern. 2003. "Managing Ideas: Commercialization Strategies for Biotechnology." IPRIA Working Papers 01/03, Intellectual Property Research Institute of Australia, Melbourne, Australia.

Gavin, Michelle. 2007. "Africa's Restless Youth." *Current History* 106 (700): 220–26.

Gibbon, Peter, and Stefano Ponte. 2005. *Trading Down: Africa, Value Chains, and the Global Economy*. Philadelphia, PA: Temple University Press.

Gibbons, M., C. Limoges, J. H. Nowotny, P. Scott Schwartzmann, and M. Trow. 1994. *The New Production of Knowledge: Science and Research in Contemporary Societies*. London: Sage Publishers.

Gibbons, Michael. 1998. "Higher Education Relevance in the 21st Century." Human Development Network, World Bank, Washington, DC.

Gibson, John, and Osaiasi Koliniusi Fatai. 2006. "Subsidies, Selectivity and the Returns to Education in Urban Papua New Guinea." *Economics of Education Review* 25 (2): 133–46.

Gordon, Robert J. 2003. "Hi-Tech Innovation and Productivity Growth: Does Supply Create Its Own Demand?" NBER Working Paper 9437, National Bureau of Economic Research, Cambridge, MA.

———. 2004a. "Two Centuries of Economic Growth: Europe Chasing the American Frontier." NBER Working Paper 10662, National Bureau of Economic Research, Cambridge, MA.

———. 2004b. "Why Was Europe Left at the Station When America's Productivity Locomotive Departed?" NBER Working Paper 10661, National Bureau of Economic Research, Cambridge, MA.

Gore, Charles. 2007. "STI and Poverty Reduction in Least Developed Countries." Presented at the Global Forum: Building Science, Technology, and Innovation Capacity for Sustainable Development and Poverty Reduction, Washington, DC, February 13.

Graff, Gregory, David Roland-Holst, and David Zilberman. 2006. "Agricultural Biotechnology and Poverty Reduction in Low-Income Countries." *World Development* 34 (8): 1430–45.

Guarini, Giulio, Vasco Molini, and Roberta Rabellotti. 2006. "Is Korea Catching Up? An Analysis of the Labour Productivity Growth in South Korea." *Oxford Development Studies* 34 (3): 323–39.

Gunning, Jan Willem, and Taye Mengistae. 2001. "Determinants of African Manufacturing Investment: The Microeconomic Evidence." *Journal of African Economies* S2 (48): 80.

Gupta, Sanjeev, Catherine Pattillo, and Smita Wagh. 2007. "Impact of Remittances on Poverty and Financial Development in Sub-Saharan Africa." IMF Working Paper WP/07/38, International Monetary Fund, Washington, DC.

Gyekye, Kwame. 2002. "A Vision of Postgraduate Education in Ghana," National Council for Tertiary Education, Accra, Ghana.

Haacker, Markus, ed. 2007. *The Macroeconomics of HIV/AIDS*. New York: Oxford University Press.

Hagmann, Jürgen, and Conny Almekinders. 2003. "Developing 'Soft Skills' in Higher Education." *Participatory Learning and Action* (48): 21–28.

Hall, Bronwyn, and Alessandro Maffioli. 2008. "Evaluating the Impact of Technology Development Funds in Emerging Economies: Evidence From Latin America." NBER Working Paper 13835, National Bureau of Economic Research, Cambridge, MA.

Hanushek, Eric A., and Ludger Woessmann. 2007. "The Role of Education Quality in Economic Growth." World Bank Policy Research Working Paper 4122, World Bank, Washington, DC.

Hassan, Mohamed H.A. 2007. "Strengthening African Universities for Science-Based Sustainable Development." Presented at the Conference on Changing Roles of Higher Education in a Globalized World, Tokyo, August 29.

Hayward, Fred M., and Daniel J. Ncayiyana. 2003. *A Guide to Strategic Planning for African Higher Education Institutions.* Pretoria, South Africa: Centre for Higher Education Transformation.

Heckman, James J. 2002. "China's Investment in Human Capital." NBER Working Paper 9296, National Bureau of Economic Research, Cambridge, MA.

Hesse, Heiko. 2006. "Export Diversification and Economic Growth," World Bank, Washington, DC.

Howells, Jeremy. 2006. "Intermediation and the Role of Intermediaries in Innovation." *Research Policy* 35 (5): 715–28.

Huisman, Jeroen, Lynn Meek, and Fiona Wood. 2007. "Institutional Diversity in Higher Education: A Cross-National and Longitudinal Analysis." *Higher Education Quarterly* 61(4): 563–77.

Hulten, Charles R. 1996. "Infrastructure Capital and Economic Growth: How Well You Use IT May Be More Important Than How Much You Have." NBER Working Paper 5847, National Bureau of Economic Research, Cambridge, MA.

Hummels, David, Jun Ishii, and Kei-Mu Yi. 2001. "The Nature and Growth of Vertical Specialization in World Trade." *Journal of International Economics* 54 (1): 75–96.

Humphrey, John, and Olga Memedovic. 2006. "Global Value Chains in the Agrifood Sector." UNIDO Working Papers, United Nations Industrial Development Organization, Vienna, Austria.

Humphreys, Macartan, Jeffrey D. Sachs, and Joseph E. Stiglitz, ed. 2007. *Escaping the Resource Curse (Initiative for Policy Dialogue at Columbia).* New York: Columbia University Press.

ICHEFAP (Center for International Higher Education). 2007. State University of New York at Buffalo. Ghana Profile. http://www.gse.buffalo.edu/org/IntHigherEdFinance/CountryProfiles/Africa/Ghana.pdf.

IFAD (International Fund for Agricultural Development) Africa. 2008. http://www. ifad.org/events/remittances/maps/africa.htm.

Imbs, Jean, and Romain Wacziarg. 2003. "Stages of Diversification." *American Economic Review* 93 (1): 63–86.

InterAcademy Council. 2004. *Realizing the Promise and Potential of African Agriculture.* Amsterdam: InterAcademy Council.

Ishengoma, Johnson. 2004. "Cost Sharing in Higher Education in Tanzania: Fact or Fiction." *Journal of Higher Education in Africa* 2 (2): 101–34.

J.E. Austin Associates. 2007. "Using Value Chain Approaches in Agribusiness and Agriculture in Sub-Saharan Africa," World Bank, Washington, DC.

Jimenez, Emmanuel Y., and Mamta Murthi. 2006. "Investing in the Youth Bulge." *Finance and Development* 43 (3): 40–43.

Johanson, Richard K., and Arvil V. Adams. 2004. "Skills Development in Sub-Saharan Africa," World Bank, Washington, DC.

Johns Hopkins Malaria Research Institute. 2007. "About Malaria." http://malaria.jhsph.edu/about_malaria.

Johnson, Simon, Jonathan D. Ostry, and Arvind Subramanian. 2007. "The Prospects for Sustained Growth in Africa: Benchmarking the Constraints." IMF Working Papers WP/07/52, International Monetary Fund, Washington, DC.

Johnstone, D. Bruce. 2004. "Higher Education Finance and Accessibility: Tuition Fees and Student Loans in Sub-Saharan Africa." *Journal of Higher Education in Africa* 2 (2): 11–36.

———. 2006. *Financing Higher Education: Cost-Sharing in International Perspective*. Rotterdam, the Netherlands: Sense Publishers.

Jorgenson, Dale W., and Kevin J. Stiroh. 2000. "Raising the Speed Limit: U.S. Economic Growth in the Information Age." OECD Working Papers, Organisation for Economic Co-operation and Development, Paris.

K-Rep Advisory Services. 2005. "Job Market Surveys, TNA, Tracer Studies for Undergraduate Degree Programmes," Sokoine University of Agriculture, Morogoro, Tanzania.

Kaijage, Erasmus S. 2007. "A Survey on the University-Industry Linkage in Tanzania and Its Impact on the Country's Economic Development," World Bank, Washington, DC.

Kaiser, Frans, Harm Hillegers, and Iwen Legro. 2005. *Lining Up Higher Education: Trends in Selected Statistics in Ten Western Countries*. Twente, the Netherlands: Centre for Higher Education Policy Studies.

Kalemli-Ozcan, Sebnem. 2006. "AIDS, Reversal of the Demographic Transition and Economic Development: Evidence from Africa." NBER Working Paper 12181, National Bureau of Economic Research, Cambridge, MA.

Kapur, Devesh, and Megan Crowley. 2008. "Beyond the ABCs: Higher Education and Developing Countries." Center for Global Development Working Paper No. 139, Washington, DC.

Karran, Terence. 2007. "Academic Freedom in Europe: A Preliminary Comparative Analysis." *Higher Education Policy* 20 (4): 289–313.

Kearney, Mary-Louise and Jeroen Huisman. 2007. "Main Transformation, Challenges and Emerging Patterns in Higher Education Systems." *Higher Education Policy* 20 (4): 361–63.

Kiamba, Crispus. 2004. "The Experience of the Privately Sponsored Studentship and Other Income Generating Activities at the University of Nairobi." *Journal of Higher Education in Africa* 2 (2): 53–74.

Kibwika, P., and J. Hagmann. 2007. "Moving From Teaching to Learning in Universities: Implications for Competence and Management." Paper presented at the biennial conference of the Regional Universities Forum for Capacity Building in Agriculture, Mangochi, Malawi, April 22–28.

Kimenyi, Mwangi S., Germano Mwabu, and Damiano Kulundu Manda. 2006. "Human Capital Externalities and Private Returns to Education in Kenya." *Eastern Economic Journal* 32 (3): 493–514.

Kjollerstrom, Monica, and Kledia Dallto. 2007. "Natural Resource-Based Industries: Prospects for Africa's Agriculture." In *Industrial Development for the 21st Century: Sustainable Development Priorities*, ed. United Nations, Department of Economic and Social Affairs, 119–81. New York: United Nations.

Kodama, Toshihiro. 2008. "The Role of Intermediation and Absorptive Capacity in Facilitating University-Industry Linkages: An Empirical Study of TAMA in Japan." *Research Policy.*

Kokkelenberg, Edward C., Michael Dillon, and Sean M. Christy. 2008. "The Effects of Class Size on Student Grades at a Public University." *Economics of Education Review* 27 (2): 221–33.

Krueger, Alan B., and Mikael Lindahl. 2001. "Education for Growth: Why and For Whom?" *Journal of Economic Literature* 39 (4): 1101–36.

Kruss, Glenda, and Jo Lorentzen. 2007. "University-Industry Linkages for Development: The Case of Western Cape Province, South Africa," World Bank, Washington, DC.

Laing, M. 2006. "Regional Agricultural Education and Training Initiatives: University of KwaZulu-Natal Experiences in Plant Breeding." Presented at the Workshop on Post-Secondary Regional Agricultural Education Training in Africa, Pietermaritzburg, South Africa, November 6.

Lao, Christine. 2007. "The Legal Constraints on University Autonomy and Accountability in Sub-Saharan Africa," African Human Development Department, World Bank, Washington, DC.

Laredo, Philippe. 2007. "Revisiting the Third Mission of Universities: Toward a Renewed Categorization of University Activities." *Higher Education Policy* 20 (4): 441–56.

Lederman, Daniel, and William F. Maloney. 2003. "R&D and Development." World Bank Policy Research Working Paper 3024, World Bank, Washington, DC.

Ledoux, B. and Alain Mingat. 2008. *La Soutenabilité Financière Comme Référence Pour Le Développement De L'Éducation Post-Primaire Dans Les Pays D'Afrique Subsaharienne.* Washington, DC: Agence Française de Développement et Banque Mondiale.

Lee, J., and H. N. Win. 2004. "Technology Transfer Between University Research Centers and Industry in Singapore." *Technovation* 24 (5): 433–42.

Lee, Jong-Wee. 2006. "Economic Growth and Human Development in the Republic of Korea, 1945–1992." Occasional Papers 24, United Nations Development Programme, New York.

Lemieux, Thomas. 2007. "Post-Secondary Education and Increasing Wage Inequality." NBER Working Paper 12077, National Bureau of Economic Research, Cambridge, MA.

Levy, Stephanie. 2007. "Public Investment to Reverse Dutch Disease: The Case of Chad." *Journal of African Economies* 16 (3): 439–84.

Lin, Tin Chun. 2004. "The Role of Higher Education in Economic Development: An Empirical Study of Taiwan Case." *Journal of Asian Economics* 15 (2): 355–71.

Lowell, B. Lindsay. 2003. "Skilled Migration Abroad or Human Capital Flight?" Migration Policy Institute. http://www.migrationinformation.org/Feature/display.cfm?ID=135.

Luhanga, Matthew L. 2003a. *Strategic Planning and Higher Education Management in Africa: The University of Dar Es Salaam Experience.* Dar es Salaam, Tanzania: University of Dar es Salaam Press.

———. 2003b. "The Tanzanian Experience in Initiating and Sustaining Tertiary Education Reform." Presented at the Africa Regional Training Conference, Improving Tertiary Education in Sub-Saharan Africa: Things That Work! Accra, Ghana, September 23.

Lundvall, Bengt-Ake. 2007. "Higher Education, Innovation and Economic Development." Presented at the World Bank's Regional Bank Conference on Development Economies, Beijing, China, January 16.

Lutz, Wolfgang, Jesus Crespo Cuaresma, and Warren Sanderson. 2008. "The Demography of Educational Attainment and Economic Growth." *Science* 319 (5866): 1047–48.

Lyakurwa, William M. 2004. "Building Human Capacity in Africa Through Networking: the AERC Example." African Economic Research Consortium. www.ifpri.org/2020africaconference/program/day2summaries/lyakurwa.pdf.

Malaria Research and Training Center (MRTC). 2005. "Initiative Universitare Pour Le Developpement De Capacité De Recherche Africaine Sur Les Maladies Tropicales," Malaria Research and Training Center and Université de Bamako, Bamako, Mali.

Mario, Mouzinho, Peter Fry, Lisbeth Levey, and Arlindo Chilundo. 2003. *Higher Education in Mozambique: A Case Study.* Oxford, UK: James Currey.

Mashelkar, Ramesh. 2007. "Scientific and Technological Opportunities and Challenges for Development." Presented at the Global Forum: Building Science, Technology, and Innovation Capacity for Sustainable Development and Poverty Reduction, Washington, DC, February 13.

Materu, Peter. 2007. "Higher Education Quality Assurance in Sub-Saharan Africa: Status, Challenges, Opportunities and Promising Practices." World Bank Working Paper No. 124, Africa Region Human Development Department, World Bank, Washington, DC.

Mazeran, Jacques, William Experton, Christian Forestier, André Gauron, Serge Goursaud, Albert Preévos, Jamil Salmi, and Francis Steier. 2007. *Short-Term Vocational Higher Education*. Paris: Hachette Education.

McMorrow, Kieran, and Werner Roger. 2007. "An Analysis of EU Growth Trends, With a Particular Focus on Germany, France, Italy and the U.K." *National Institute Economic Review* 199 (1): 82–98.

Menon, Maria Eliophotou. 2008. "Perceived Rates of Return to Higher Education: Further Evidence From Cyprus." *Economics of Education Review* 27 (1): 39–47.

Mihyo, Paschal B. 2008. "Staff Retention in African Universities and Links with Diaspora Study." Presented at Association for the Development of Education in Africa (ADEA) Biennial Conference on Beyond Primary Education, Maputo, Mozambique, May 5.

Mingat, Alain, and Kirsten Majgaard. 2008. "A Cross-Country Study of Education in Sub-Saharan Africa," World Bank: Washington, DC.

Mingat, Alain, Blandine Ledoux, and Ramahatra Rakotomalala. 2008. "Financial Sustainability as a Reference for the Development of Post-Primary Education in Sub-Saharan Africa." Presented at ADEA Biennial Conference on Beyond Primary Education, Maputo, Mozambique, May 5.

Ministry of Education of Ethiopia. 2005. *Education Statistics Annual Abstract 2004/2005*. Addis Ababa: Ministry of Education.

Mkude, Daniel, and Abel G. Ishumi. 2004. *Tracer Studies in a Quest for Academic Improvement: The Process and Results of a University-Wide Tracer Study Project Conducted in 2002–2003*. Dar es Salaam, Tanzania: Dar es Salaam University Press.

Mohrman, Kathryn, Wanhua Ma, and David Baker. 2008. "The Research University in Transition: The Emerging Global Model." *Higher Education Policy* 21 (1): 5–27.

Mokopakgosi, Brian. 2006. "A Survey of Academic Staff Retention at the University of Botswana," University of Botswana, Gaborone.

Montgomery, John D. and Dennis A. Rondinelli, eds. 1995. *Great Policies: Strategic Innovations in Asia and the Pacific Basin*. Westport, CT: Praeger.

Mouton, Johann. 2008. "Study on National Research Systems: a Meta-Review." Presented at the UNESCO Symposium on Comparative Analysis of National Research Systems, Paris, January 16.

Mugabushaka, Alexis-Michel, Harald Schomburg, and Ulrich Teichler, ed. 2007. *Higher Education and Work in Africa*. Kassel, Germany: International Centre for Higher Education Research.

Muir-Leresche, Kay. 2006. *Improving Approaches for Effective Teaching and Learning: Tertiary Agricultural Education*. Nairobi, Kenya: World Agroforestry Centre.

Mullan, Fitzhugh. 2005. "The Metrics of the Physician Brain Drain." *The New England Journal of Medicine* 353 (17): 1810–18.

Musisi, Nakanyike B., and Nansozi K. Muwanga. 2003. *Makerere University in Transition: 1993–2000*. Oxford, UK: James Currey.

The Nation (Kenya). 2004. "Malaria Herb Now Turns Top Cash Crop," December 16.

National Center for Education Statistics. 2004. *Highlights from the Trends in International Mathematics and Science Study (TIMSS) 2003*. Washington, DC: U.S. Department of Education.

National Universities Commission. 2002. "Academic Staffing Profiles, Student Enrollment, Dropout and Graduation Rates at Nigerian Universities during 1995/96 to 1999/2000 Academic Years," Department of Academic Planning, National Universities Commission, Abuja, Nigeria.

Ndulu, Benno. 2004. "Human Capital Flight: Stratification, Globalization, and the Challenges to Tertiary Education in Africa," World Bank, Washington, DC.

———. 2007. "Facing the Challenges of African Growth: Opportunities, Constraints, and Strategic Directions," World Bank, Washington, DC.

Ndulu, Benno, Lopamudra Chakraborti, Lebohang Lijane, Vijaya Ramachandran, and Jerome Wolgin. 2007. *Challenges of African Growth: Opportunities, Constraints, and Strategic Directions*. Washington, DC: World Bank.

Nelson, Richard R., ed. 1993. *National Innovation Systems: A Comparative Analysis*. New York: Oxford University Press.

Ng'ethe, Njuguna, and Charles Ngome. 2007. "University-Industry Linkages in Kenya: With Special Reference to the Jomo Kenyatta University of Agriculture and Technology (JKUAT)," World Bank," Washington, DC.

Ng'ethe, Njuguna, George Subotzky, and George Afeti. 2007. "Differentiation and Articulation in Tertiary Education Systems: A Study of Selected African Countries." Africa Human Development Series, World Bank, Washington, DC.

Nordhaus, William D. 2001. "Productivity Growth and the New Economy." NBER Working Paper 8096, National Bureau of Economic Research, Cambridge, MA.

Noriega, Maria del Pilar. 2007. "The Role of a Technological Development Center: Lessons for Success." Presented at the Global Forum: Building Science, Technology, and Innovation Capacity for Sustainable Development and Poverty Reduction, Washington, DC, February 13.

Nunn, Nathan. 2007. "Historical Legacies: A Model Linking Africa's Past to Its Current Underdevelopment." *Journal of Development Economics* 83 (1): 157–75.

O'Hare, Daniel. 2006. "Education in Ireland: 1960–2000," Organisation for Economic Co-operation and Development, Paris.

O'Neil, Kevin. 2003. "Brain Drain and Gain: the Case of Taiwan." Migration Policy Institute. http://www.migrationinformation.org/Feature/display.cfm?ID=155.

OAU (Organization of African Unity). 1990. *The Lagos Plan of Action for the Economic Development of Africa: 1980–2000.* Addis Ababa: Organization of African Unity.

OECD (Organisation for Economic Co-Operation and Development). 2006. *Evolution of Student Interest in Science and Technology Studies Policy Report.* Paris: Organisation for Economic Co-operation and Development.

Okebukola, Peter, Suleiman Ramon-Yusuf, and Abdulrahaman Sambo. 2007. "Cost-Benefit Analysis of Accreditation: Case Study of Nigeria," National Universities Commission, Abuja, Nigeria.

Oluoch-Kosura, W. 2006. "Agricultural Education and Training in Sub-Saharan Africa: Experiences of the Collaborative Master of Science in Agricultural and Applied Economics (CMAAE)." Presented at the Workshop on Post-Secondary Regional Agricultural Education Training in Africa, Pietermaritzburg, South Africa, November 6.

Oni, Bankole. 2005. "Labour Market Requirements and the Nigerian Graduate." In *Perspectives and Reflections on Nigerian Higher Education,* ed. Munzali Jibril, Munzali 119–38. Ibadan, Nigeria: Spectrum Books.

Ono, Hiroshi. 2007. "Does Examination Hell Pay Off? A Cost-Benefit Analysis of 'Ronin' and College Education in Japan." *Economics of Education Review* 26 (3): 271–84.

Otieno, Wycliffe. 2004. "Student Loans in Kenya: Past Experiences, Current Hurdles and Opportunities for the Future." *Journal of Higher Education in Africa* 2 (2): 75–100.

Oxford Analytica. 2008a. "China: Fertilizer Follows Food Price Control," January 23.

———. 2008b. "International: Food Crisis Leads to Trade Restrictions," April 2.

———. 2008c. "International: Rice Rise May Mark Growing Food Crisis," March 28.

———. 2008d. "International: Wheat's Dramatic Rise Demands Response," February 28.

Oyelaran-Oyeyinka, Banji, and Boladale Abiola. 2007. "University-Industry Linkage in Nigeria," World Bank, Washington, DC.

Paarlberg, Robert. 2008. *Starved for Science: How Biotechnology Is Being Kept Out of Africa.* Cambridge, MA: Harvard University Press.

Page, John, and Sonia Plaza. 2006. "Migration Remittances and Development: A Review of Global Evidence." *Journal of African Economies* 15 (S2): 245–336.

Pan, Su-Yan. 2007. "Intertwining of Academia and Officialdom and University Autonomy: Experience From Tsinghua University in China." *Higher Education Policy* 20 (4): 121–44.

Porter, Michael. 1990. *The Competitive Advantage of Nations*. New York: Free Press.

Pritchett, Lant. 2001. "Where Has All the Education Gone?" *The World Bank Economic Review* 15 (3): 367–91.

PROPHE (Program for Research On Private Higher Education). 2007. "Country Data Summary: 2000–2006," State University of New York at Albany, Albany, NY.

Psacharopoulos, George. 2006. "The Value of Investment in Education: Theory, Evidence, and Policy." *Journal of Education Finance* 32 (2): 113–36.

Psacharopoulos, George, and Harry Anthony Patrinos. 2004. "Returns to Investment in Education: A Further Update." *Education Economics* 12 (2): 111–34.

Rasiah, Rajah. 2006. "Explaining Malaysia's Export Expansion in Palm Oil and Related Products." In *Technology, Adaptation, and Exports: How Some Developing Countries Got It Right*, ed. Vandana Chandra, 163–92. Washington, DC: World Bank.

Raynolds, Laura T. 2004. "The Globalization of Organic Agro-Food Networks." *World Development* 32 (5): 725–43.

Rhoades, G. 1990. "Political Competition and Differentiation in Higher Education," In *Differentiation Theory and Social Change*, ed. J.C. Alexander and P. Colony. New York: Columbia University Press.

Richardson, Geoffrey, and John Fielden. 1997. *Measuring the Grip of the State: A Study of the Relationships Between Governments and Universities in Selected Commonwealth Countries*. London: Commonwealth Higher Education Management Service.

Robb, David, and Bin Xie. 2003. "A Survey of Manufacturing Strategy and Technology in the Chinese Furniture Industry." *European Management Journal* 21 (4): 484–96.

Rodrik, Dani. 2006. "Understanding South Africa's Economic Puzzles." NBER Working Paper 12565, National Bureau of Economic Research, Cambridge, MA.

———. 2007. *One Economics, Many Recipes: Globalization, Institutions, and Economic Growth*. Princeton, NJ: Princeton University Press.

Romer, Paul M. 2000. "Should the Government Subsidize Supply or Demand in the Market for Scientists and Engineers?" NBER Working Paper 7723, National Bureau of Economic Research, Cambridge, MA.

Saint, William. 1992. "Universities in Africa: Strategies for Stabilization and Revitalization." World Bank Technical Paper 194, World Bank, Washington, DC.

———. 2006. *Innovation Funds for Higher Education: A User's Guide for World Bank Funded Projects*. Washington, DC: World Bank.

Salisu, Mohammed. 2005. "The Role of Capital Flight and Remittances in Current Account Sustainability in Sub-Saharan Africa." *African Development Review* 17 (3): 382–404.

Salmi, Jamil. 1999. "Student Loans in an International Perspective: the World Bank Experience." LCSHD Working Paper 44, World Bank, Washington, DC.

———. 2007. "Autonomy From the State Vs. Responsiveness to Markets." *Higher Education Policy* 20 (4): 223–42.

———. 2008. "The Challenges of Establishing World-Class Universities." HDNED. Washington, DC, World Bank.

Salmi, Jamil, and Arthur M. Hauptman. 2006. "Innovations in Tertiary Education Financing: A Comparative Evaluation of Allocation Mechanisms." Education Working Paper Series 4, World Bank, Washington, DC.

Sambo, A.S. 2005. "The Role of Science and Technology Training Institutions in Socio-Economic Development." Presented at the First African Conference of Vice-Chancellors, Provosts and Deans of Science, Engineering and Technology, Accra, Ghana, November 15.

Savery, John R., and Thomas M. Duffy. 2001. "Problem Based Learning: An Instructional Model and Its Constructivist Framework." CRLT Technical Report 16-01, Center for Research on Learning and Technology, Indiana University, Bloomington, IN.

Sawyerr, Akilagpa. 2004. "African Universities and the Challenge of Research Capacity Development." *Journal of Higher Education in Africa* 2 (1): 213–42.

Saxenian, AnnaLee. 2006. *The New Argonauts.* Cambridge, MA: Harvard University Press.

Schady, Norbert. 2003. "Convexity and Sheepskin Effects in the Human Capital Earnings Function: Recent Evidence for Filipino Men." *Oxford Bulletin of Economics and Statistics* 65 (2): 171–96.

Schultz, T. Paul. 2004. "Evidence of Returns to Schooling in Africa from Household Surveys: Monitoring and Restructuring the Market for Education." *Journal of African Economies* 13 (S2): ii95–ii148.

Schultz, Theodore W. 1975. "The Value of the Ability to Deal With Disequilibria." *Journal of Economic Literature* 13 (3): 827–46.

Science. 2007. "Empowering Green Chemists," June 29.

Seo, Sungno Niggol, and Robert Mendelson. 2007. "Climate Change Adaptation in Africa: A Microeconomic Analysis of Livestock Choice." World Bank Policy Research Working Paper 4277, World Bank, Washington, DC.

Shabani, Juma. 2006. "Higher Education in French-Speaking Sub-Saharan Africa." In *International Handbook for Higher Education*, ed. James J.F. Forest and Philip G. Altbach, the Netherlands: Springer.

Silles, Mary A. 2007. "The Returns to Education for the United Kingdom." *Journal of Applied Economics* 10 (1): 391–413.

Solimano, Andrés. 2002. "Globalizing Talent and Human Capital: Implications for Developing Countries." Presented at the Fourth Annual Bank Conference on Development Economics for Europe, Oslo, Norway, June 24.

Solow, Robert. 2001. "Information Technology and the Recent Productivity Boom in the U.S." Presented at the Cambridge-MIT National Competitiveness Summit 2001, Cambridge, MA, November.

Sonu, Jungho. 2007. "Imitation to Internalization: the Case of Korea." *Development Outreach* (June): 10–13.

Stark, Oded, and C. Simon Fan. 2007. "Losses and Gains to Developing Countries From the Migration of Educated Workers: An Overview of Recent Research, and New Reflections." *World Economics* 8 (2): 259–70.

Stern, Nicholas. 2007. *The Economics of Climate Change: The Stern Review*. Cambridge, UK: Cambridge University Press.

Stern, Scott, Michael Porter, and Jeffrey Furman. 2000. "The Determinants of National Innovative Capacity." NBER Working Paper 7876, National Bureau for Economic Research, Cambridge, MA.

Tanzania Education Authority. 2007. *Annual Report 2006*. Dar es Salaam, Tanzania: Ministry of Higher Education, Science and Technology.

Tanzania Ministry of Science, Technology and Higher Education. 2004. *Medium Term Strategic Plan: 2004–2007*. Dar es Salaam, Tanzania: Tanzania Ministry of Higher Education, Science and Technology.

Task Force on Higher Education and Society. 2000. *Higher Education in Developing Countries: Peril and Promise*. Washington, DC: World Bank.

Teferra, Damtew, and Philip G. Altbach, ed. 2003. *African Higher Education: An International Reference Handbook*. Bloomington, IN: Indiana University Press.

Tekleselassie, Abebayehu. 2002. "Cost-Sharing in Higher Education in Ethiopia: Demystifying the Myth." International Comparative Higher Education Finance and Accessibility Project Discussion Paper. Graduate School of Education, University of Buffalo, Buffalo, NY.

Tettey, Wisdom. 2006. "Staff Retention in African Universities: Elements of a Sustainable Strategy," World Bank, Washington, DC.

Thomas, Harold G. 1999. "Developing a Strategic Plan: A Case Study From the National University of Lesotho." *Higher Education Policy* 11 (2/3): 235–43.

Thorn, Kristian, Lauritz Holm-Nielsen, and Jette Samuel Jeppeson. 2004. "Approaches to Results Based Funding in Tertiary Education: Identifying Finance Reform Options for Chile." World Bank Policy Research Working Paper 3436, World Bank, Washington, DC.

Thurow, L. 1999. *Building Wealth: New Rules for Individuals, Companies and Nations in a Knowledge-Based Economy*. New York: Harper Business.

Tongoona, P., and M. Mudhara. 2007. "Regional Training Strategies for Post-Secondary Agricultural Education in Sub-Saharan Africa: When Do They Work and How Should They Be Done," World Bank: Washington, DC.

Trinidade, Sergio. 2007. "Public-Private Partnerships in Science and Technology Capacity Building." Presented at the Global Forum: Building Science, Technology, and Innovation Capacity for Sustainable Development and Poverty Reduction, Washington, DC, February 13.

Trow, M. 1974. *Problems in the Transition from Elite to Mass Higher Education*. Paris: Organisation for Economic Co-operation and Development.

Tusubira, F. F., and Ali Ndiwalana. 2007. "University-Industry Linkages for Development: The Case of Uganda," World Bank, Washington, DC.

UNCTAD (United Nations Conference on Trade and Development). 2007. *The Least Developed Countries Report*. Geneva: United Nations.

UNESCO (United Nations Educational, Scientific and Cultural Organization). 2005. *Experiences with Technical and Vocational Education and Training*. Paris: UNESCO.

———. 2007. *Education for All by 2015: Will We Make It?* Paris: UNESCO.

UNESCO Global Education Digest. 2007. "Comparing Education Statistics Across the World", Institute for Statistics, Montreal.

UNIDO (United Nations Industrial Development Organization). 2004. "Industrial Development in Sub-Saharan Africa." In *Industrial Development Report 2004: Industrialization, Environment and the Millennium Development Goals in Sub-Saharan Africa*, ed. UNIDO, 29–72. Vienna: UNIDO.

———. 2005. *Industrial Development Report 2005*. Vienna, Austria: UNIDO.

University World News. 2007. "Massachusetts Signs Ground-Breaking China Deal," April 6.

———. 2008a. "Australia: Universities—the New Polytechnics," April 13.

———. 2008b. "UK: End of the British Binary System," April 13.

———. 2008c. "New Zealand: Polytechnic Universities Opposed," April 13.

Urdal, Henrik. 2006. "A Clash of Generations? Youth Bulges and Political Violence." *International Studies Quarterly* 50 (3): 607–29.

Van Harte, Meagan. 2002. "Can Student Loan Schemes Ensure Access to Higher Education: South Africa's Experience." International Comparative Higher Education Finance and Accessibility Project Discussion Paper, Graduate School of Education, University of Buffalo, Buffalo, NY.

Van Vught, Frans. 2007. "Diversity and Differentiation in Higher Education Systems." Paper presented at the 10th Anniversary Conference of the Centre for Higher Education Transformation, Johannesberg, South Africa.

Varghese, N.V. 2008. "State, Markets, Faith and Proliferation of Private Higher Education in Africa." Presented at the 2008 Biannual Conference of the

Association for the Development of Education in Africa, United Nations Educational, Scientific and Cultural Organization, Paris.

Wagner, Joachim. 2007. "Exports and Productivity: A Survey of the Evidence From Firm-Level Data." *The World Economy* 30 (1): 60–82.

Watson, Robert T., Marufu C. Zinyowera, and Richard H. Moss. 2007. *IPCC Special Report on the Regional Impacts of Climate Change: An Assessment of Vulnerability.* World Meteorological Organization (WMO); The United Nations Environment Programme (UNEP).

Weir, Sharada, and John Knight. 2007. "Production Externalities of Education: Evidence From Rural Ethiopia." *Journal of African Economies* 16 (1): 134–65.

Wondimu, Habtamu. 2003. "Ethiopia." In *African Higher Education: An International Reference Handbook,* ed. Damtew Teferra and Philip G. Altbach, 316–32. Bloomington, IN: Indiana University Press.

Wood, A. 1994. *North-South Trade, Employment and Inequality: Changing Fortunes in a Skilled-Driven World.* Oxford, UK: Oxford University Press.

Wood, A., and K. Berge. 1997. "Exporting Manufactures: Human Resources, Natural Resources, and Trade Policy." *Journal of Development Studies* 34 (35): 39.

Wood, A., and J. Mayer. 2001. "Africa's Export Structure in a Comparative Perspective." *Cambridge Journal of Economics* 25 (369): 394.

Woodhall, Maureen. 2007. "Funding Higher Education: The Contribution of Economic Thinking to Debate and Policy Development." Education Working Paper Series 78, World Bank, Washington, DC.

World Bank. 1988. *Education in Sub-Saharan Africa: Policies for Adjustment, Revitalization and Expansion.* Washington, DC: World Bank.

———. 1991a. *The African Capacity Building Initiative: Toward Improved Policy Analysis and Development Management.* Washington, DC: World Bank.

——— 1991b. "Vocational and Technical Education and Training." World Bank Policy Papers, World Bank, Washington, DC.

———. 1994. *World Development Report 1994.* Washington, DC: World Bank.

———. 1999. *World Development Report 1998/1999: Knowledge for Development.* New York: Oxford University Press.

———. 2002. *Constructing Knowledge Societies: New Challenges for Tertiary Education.* Washington, DC: World Bank.

———. 2003. *Higher Education Development for Ethiopia: Pursuing the Vision.* Washington, DC: World Bank.

———. 2004a. "Cost, Financing and School Effectiveness in Malawi: Country Status Report." Africa Region Human Development Department Working Paper 78, World Bank, Washington, DC.

———. 2004b. "Strengthening the Foundation of Education and Training in Kenya." Report No. 28064-KE, World Bank, Washington, DC.

————. 2005. "Primary and Secondary Education in Lesotho: a Country Status Report." Africa Region Human Development Department Working Paper 101, World Bank, Washington, DC.

————. 2006a. "Nigeria: Science and Technology Education at the Post-Basic Level." Africa Region Human Development Department, Report No. 37973, World Bank, Washington, DC.

————. 2006b. *World Development Indicators, 2006.* Washington, DC: World Bank.

————. 2007a. "Le Système Éducatif Burundais: Diagnostic Et Perspectives Pour Une Nouvelle Politique Éducatif Dans Le Context De L'Éducation Primaire Gratuite Pour Tous," World Bank, Washington, DC.

————. 2007b. "Le Système Éducatif Tchadien: Eléments De Diagnostic Pour Une Politique Éducatif Nouvelle Et Une Meilleure Efficacité De La Dépense Publique," World Bank, Washington, DC.

————. 2007c. *World Development Report 2007: Development and the Next Generation.* Washington, DC: World Bank.

————. 2008a. *At the Crossroads: Challenges for Secondary Education in Sub-Saharan Africa.* Washington, DC: World Bank.

————. 2008b. "Closing the Skill Gap: The Role of Education Supporting Growth and Competitiveness in the ECA Region," World Bank, Washington, DC.

————. 2008c. *Costs and Financing of Higher Education in Francophone Africa.* Washington, DC: World Bank.

————. 2008d. "Higher Education in Francophone Africa: What Tools Can Be Used to Support Financially-Sustainable Policies." World Bank Working Paper 135, World Bank, Washington, DC.

————. 2008e. *Migration and Remittances Factbook 2008.* Washington, DC: World Bank.

————. 2008f. "Rising Food Prices: Policy Options and World Bank Response." Background note for the Development Committee, World Bank, Washington, DC.

World Bank Institute. 2007. *Building Knowledge Economies.* Washington, DC: World Bank.

Yang, Deninis Tao. 2005. "Determinants of Schooling Returns During Transition: Evidence From Chinese Cities." *Journal of Comparative Economics* 33 (2): 244–64.

Yesufu, T. M. 1973. *Creating the African University: Emerging Issues of the 1970s.* Ibadan, Nigeria: Oxford University Press.

Yizengaw, Teshome. 2006. "Cost Sharing in the Ethiopian Higher Education System: the Need, Implications, and Future Directions." Paper prepared for the International Comparative Higher Education Finance and Accessibility Project at SUNY/Buffalo, Buffalo, NY. www.gse.buffalo.edu/org/inthighered-finance/publications.html.

Yusuf, Shahid. 2008. "Intermediating Knowledge Exchange Between Universities and Businesses." *Research Policy* 37 (8): 1167–1174.

Yusuf, Shahid, M. Anjum Altaf, Barry Eichengreen, Sudarshan Gooptu, Kaoru Nabeshima, Charles Kenny, Dwight H. Perkins, and Marc Shotten. 2003. *Innovative East Asia: The Future of Growth.* New York: Oxford University Press.

Zeng, Douglas Zhihua, ed. 2008. *Knowledge, Technology, and Cluster-Based Growth in Africa.* Washington, DC: World Bank.

Background Studies

Basant, Rakesh, and Pankaj Chandra. 2006. "Linking Technical Education to Business Growth: A Case Study on Building Technical Skills in India," Indian Institute of Management, Ahmedabad.

Bloom, David, David Canning, and Kevin Chan. 2006. "Higher Education and Economic Development in Africa." Africa Region Human Development Department No. 102, World Bank, Washington, DC.

Brossard, Mathieu, and Borel Foko. 2007. "Coûts Et Financement De L'Enseignement Supérieur En Afrique Francophone." Africa Region Human Development Department, Washington, DC: World Bank.

Bunwaree, Sheila, and Sanjeev K. Sobhee. 2007. "University-Industry Linkages: The Case of Mauritius," World Bank, Washington, DC.

Chandra, Vandana, Jessica Boccardo, and I. Osorio. 2007. "Export Diversification and Competitiveness in Developing Countries," World Bank, Washington, DC.

Darvas, Peter. 2007. "Tertiary Education in Sub-Saharan Africa: An Overview," Africa Region Human Development Department, World Bank, Washington, DC.

Essegbey, George O. 2007. "University-Industry Linkages in Africa: The Ghana Case Study," World Bank, Washington, DC.

Kaijage, Erasmus S. 2007. "A Survey on the University-Industry Linkage in Tanzania and Its Impact on the Country's Economic Development," World Bank, Washington, DC.

Kruss, Glenda, and Jo Lorentzen. 2007. "University-Industry Linkages for Development: The Case of Western Cape Province, South Africa," World Bank, Washington, DC.

Materu, Peter. 2007. "Higher Education Quality Assurance in Sub-Saharan Africa: Status, Challenges, Opportunities and Promising Practices." Africa Region Human Development Department, World Bank, Washington, DC.

Ng'ethe, Njuguna, and Charles Ngome. 2007. "University-Industry Linkages in Kenya: With Special Reference to the Jomo Kenyatta University of Agriculture and Technology (JKUAT)," World Bank, Washington, DC.

Oyelaran-Oyeyinka, Banji, and Boladale Abiola. 2007. "University-Industry Linkage in Nigeria," World Bank, Washington, DC.

Tettey, Wisdom. 2006. "Staff Retention in African Universities: Elements of a Sustainable Strategy," World Bank, Washington, DC.

Tusubira, F.F., and Ali Ndiwalana. 2007. "University-Industry Linkages for Development: The Case of Uganda," World Bank, Washington, DC.

World Bank. 2006. "Nigeria: Science and Technology Education at the Post-Basic Level." Report No. 37973, Africa Region Human Development Department, World Bank, Washington, DC.

Index

Figures, notes, and tables are indicated by f, n, and t, respectively.

ECO-AUDIT
Environmental Benefits Statement

The World Bank is committed to preserving endangered forests and natural resources. The Office of the Publisher has chosen to print *Accelerating Catch-up* on recycled paper with 30 percent postconsumer fiber in accordance with the recommended standards for paper usage set by the Green Press Initiative, a nonprofit program supporting publishers in using fiber that is not sourced from endangered forests. For more information, visit www.greenpressinitiative.org.

Saved:
- 7 trees
- 5 million BTUs of total energy
- 658 lbs. of net greenhouse gases
- 2731 gallons of waste water
- 351 lbs. of solid waste